How Christ Came To Church

You are holding a reproduction of an original work that is in the public domain in the United States of America, and possibly other countries. You may freely copy and distribute this work as no entity (individual or corporate) has a copyright on the body of the work. This book may contain prior copyright references, and library stamps (as most of these works were scanned from library copies). These have been scanned and retained as part of the historical artifact.

This book may have occasional imperfections such as missing or blurred pages, poor pictures, errant marks, etc. that were either part of the original artifact, or were introduced by the scanning process. We believe this work is culturally important, and despite the imperfections, have elected to bring it back into print as part of our continuing commitment to the preservation of printed works worldwide. We appreciate your understanding of the imperfections in the preservation process, and hope you enjoy this valuable book.

HOW
CHRIST CAME TO CHURCH

By Rev. A. J. Gordon, D. D.

Adoniram Judson Gordon. A Biography. By his son, Ernest B. Gordon. With portraits and other illustrations. 8vo, cloth $1.50

The Ministry of the Spirit. Introduction by Rev. F. B. Meyer, B.A. 12mo, cloth, gilt top . 1.00
CHEAP EDITION, 18mo, cloth, net, 25 c.; by post, net .30

How Christ Came to Church: The Pastor's Dream. A Spiritual Autobiography. With the life-story and the dream as interpreting the man, by Rev. A. T. Pierson, D. D. With portrait. 8vo., gilt top 75
CHEAP EDITION, 18mo, cloth, net 25c.; by post, net .30

In Christ; or, the Believer's Union with his Lord. 12mo, cloth, gilt top, $1.00; paper . . net .35
POCKET EDITION. Long 18mo, cloth 1.00
CHEAP EDITION, 18mo, cloth, net, 25c.; by post, net .30

The Holy Spirit in Missions. 12mo, cloth, gilt top 1.25

Grace and Glory. Sermons for the Life that Now is and that which is to Come. 12mo, cloth, gilt top, $1.50; paper . . . . net .50

Ecce Venit; or, Behold He Cometh. 12mo, cloth, gilt top, $1 25; paper . . . . net .50

The Ministry of Healing; or, Miracles of Cures in all Ages. With history of the doctrine from the earliest times. 12mo, cloth, gilt top . . 1.25
Paper . . . . net .50

The Two-Fold Life; or, Christ's Work for Us, and Christ's Work in Us. 12mo, cloth, gilt top, $1 25; paper . . . . net .50

Risen with Christ; or, the Resurrection of Christ and of the Believer. 16mo, boards . .30

The First Thing in the World; or, the Primacy of Faith. 16mo, Popular Vellum Series .20
CHEAP EDITION, net, 10c.; per doz. . . . . . net 1.00

The Coronation Hymnal. 400 Hymns with Music. By Rev. Drs. A. J. Gordon and A. T. Pierson. 4to, half-cloth, red edges . . . . . net .60
Cloth, red edges . . . . net .75

Two editions: An edition for general use, and a Baptist edition. Send for specimen pages.

HOW
CHRIST CAME TO CHURCH

THE PASTOR'S DREAM

A SPIRITUAL AUTOBIOGRAPHY
BY A. J. GORDON, D. D.

WITH

THE LIFE-STORY, AND THE DREAM AS INTERPRETING THE MAN
BY A. T. PIERSON, D. D.

"Lo, I am with you alway"
The Christ

FLEMING H. REVELL COMPANY
NEW YORK   CHICAGO   TORONTO
Publishers of Evangelical Literature

AMERICAN BAPTIST PUBLICATION SOCIETY
1420 Chestnut Street, Philadelphia
BOSTON   NEW YORK   CHICAGO   ST. LOUIS   DALLAS   ATLANTA
MDCCCXCVI

Copyright 1895 by the
AMERICAN BAPTIST PUBLICATION SOCIETY

CONTENTS

PART I

THE LIFE-STORY . . . . vii–xxiii

PART II

HOW CHRIST CAME TO CHURCH . . . 25–92

I. THE DREAM 27

II. HERE TO-DAY 33

III. AND TO COME AGAIN 44

IV. IF I HAD NOT COME 56

V. IN THY LIGHT 65

VI. THE TEMPLE OF GOD IS HOLY 74

VII. CLEANSING THE TEMPLE 85

PART III

THE DREAM AS INTERPRETING THE MAN 93-149

I. Loyalty to the Person of Christ . . 100

II. The Personal Coming of Christ . . . 106

III. The Sacredness of the Preacher's Vocation 113

IV. Jealousy for Divine Worship 121

V. The Authority of the Word of God 127

VI. The Scriptural Pattern of Church Life 133

VII. The Presidency of the Spirit in the Church 139

VIII. The Last Message to the Church . . 146

PART I
THE LIFE-STORY

i

THE LIFE-STORY

HOW simple and brief are the outlines of a human life. And yet only eternity can fill out those outlines, and make visible the unseen mysteries which we call character and influence.

ADONIRAM JUDSON GORDON

Was born April 19, 1836.

Was converted to God in 1852, and was baptized the same year.

Was in New London, from 1853 to 1857; in Brown University, from 1857 to 1860; in Newton Theological Seminary, from 1860 to 1863.

Ordained at Jamaica Plain, June, 1863.

Married to Maria Hale, October 13, 1863.

Removed to Boston, December, 1869.

Departed this life, February 2, 1895.

This life thus reaches over a period lacking little of three-score years, and may be roughly divided into three parts, each embracing about twenty years : the first twenty, his growth to manhood ; the second twenty, his development as a Bible student and preacher of the word ; and the third period being especially memorable for his maturity as a Spirit-filled teacher and leader.

The character and life of Dr. Gordon are so rich, both in incident and suggestion, so full of lessons in living for generations to come, that it is proposed to prepare a fuller biography hereafter. But, by way of introducing this marvelous personality to readers who were acquainted with the man only through his writings or public utterances, it may be well to give a brief sketch, as in profile, of his leading characteristics, and especially such as may help to elucidate the experiences connected with the dream, here recorded.

Dr. Gordon will long be remembered as a prince among the preachers and teachers of the modern pulpit. With preachers, as with musicians, there are different and distinct classes, and it is easy to find to which he belongs.

Some study to express the word and mind of God ; they are exegetes. Others study their own states and express their own spiritual moods and experiences ; they are autobiographers. Others deal in divine conceptions, but invest them with the interest of their own experimental history ;

these are witnesses and reach the truest ideal. Dr. Gordon was one of these. No man's preaching was a more faithful exposition of the word of God. He would have counted it an affront to the Scriptures to use them as a mere convenience to hang his own thoughts on, or caricature them by a misapplication of sacred words. He was both too original in research and too independent in opinion, to become a mere reflector of others' views, like the copyist, or substitute sound for sense like the dealer in platitudes. He honestly, patiently, and prayerfully studied the word of God, and then illustrated—we might almost say illuminated—it by his own experience.

No review of this life, however hasty, must leave out his work as an author. Ten marked contributions to the literature of the age remain, apart from the editorials and more transient articles in the "Watchword," the religious newspapers, the "Missionary Review," etc. His books fall into five classes. One on "The Ministry of Healing," another, his "Coronation Hymnal," and this last, his "Spiritual Autobiography," must stand by themselves. Then there are four precious books which center about the person of Christ: "In Christ," "The Two-fold Life," "Grace and Glory," and "Ecce Venit." Two have specially to do with the Holy Spirit: "The Ministry of the Spirit," and the "Holy Spirit in Missions." But what a wide range and scope of treatment, and on what vital themes! It is not too much to say of these books that they constitute religious classics, and ought to form part of every well-furnished library.

In his literary style three things are peculiarly prominent : first, his vigorous and discriminating use of language ; secondly, his marvelous power of analysis and antithesis ; and thirdly, his simple, natural, forceful illustrations. In these respects his writings will repay any one for critical and habitual study. If the literary productions of any man of this century can in these respects supply a better model for young men who are preparing to preach, we know not where they are to be found. Dr. Gordon's book, for instance, on the "Ministry of the Spirit," is so tersely written and so carefully wrought out in every part, that there is scarcely one needless noun or heedless adjective in all the sixty thousand words which compose it ; while every page bristles with new and instructive suggestions ; and the whole is so reverent and worshipful that it suggests a man consciously treading on holy ground.

Twenty-five years of this serviceable life were spent in the Clarendon Street Church, Boston ; and in helping to mold that church into conformity with primitive apostolic models was found the crowning work of his life. It implies neither exaggeration of his own merit nor depreciation of the service of any other man to affirm that it was permitted to him, amid the atmosphere of Unitarianism and liberalism, to build up a believing brotherhood, characterized by as simple worship, pure doctrine, and primitive practice as any other in the world.

To those who are familiar with the inner secrets of the life of this church, its central charm is one which is not apparent to the common eye : the *administration of the Holy Spirit* is there devoutly recognized and practically realized. The beloved pastor sought, and with great success, to impress upon his people the fact that in the body of Christ the Holy Spirit literally though invisibly indwells ; that he is ready, if he finds a willing people, to oversee and administer all that pertains to the affairs of the body of Christ ; and that, as his administration both demands and depends upon co-operation, there must be neither secular men nor secular methods introduced into the practical conduct of Christ's church, but the Spirit of God must be recognized and realized as the Divine Archbishop finding there his See. It took years to get this practically wrought into the life of the church ; but under his persistent teaching and patient pastoral guidance, there came a gradual elimination of worldly elements, and a gradual transformation of the whole church as a working body until it has become a model for other churches, approximating very closely to the apostolic pattern.

Dr. Gordon has written many noble books and pamphlets; but among all the volumes he has produced, this is the most complete and satisfactory. This church is his permanent "living epistle." The golden pen of action, held in the firm hand of an inspired purpose, has been for a quarter of a century writing out its sentences in living deeds, to be known and read of all men. And the greatest problem now awaiting solution is, how far this church is going to prove that the Holy Spirit still administers the body of Christ there. Should these brethren show that they have been inwardly saying, "I am of Dr. Gordon," rather than, "I am of Christ"; and were this church to prove only a sheaf, of which the pastor was the bond, and which when the bond is removed falls apart, it would be a world-wide reproach. If, on the other hand, it shall not only as an organization survive the pastor's removal, but shall preserve jealously the high type of excellence it attained under his ministry; shall prove not man-centered but Christ-centered; and shall regard itself as a kind of legatee unto whom the pastor has committed the gospel he preached, the work he began, and the witness he maintained, to be guarded and perpetuated—this survival of the whole work when the workman has gone up higher, will be a testimony to the whole church and the whole world, as mighty and as far-reaching as any witness of its sort in our generation.

It is a growing conviction that the life-work of Dr. Gordon has reached singular completeness, a rounded symmetry and sphericity. Nothing seems wanting. In the beauty of Christian character and culture he had so grown into the measure of the stature of the fullness of Christ, that it may be doubted whether the whole communion of believers presented one man more ripe in godliness and usefulness. He was in every sense a great man: great in his mind, in his genius, having not only the administrative but the creative faculty; not only organizing but originating. His versatility was amazing. He would have been great in many spheres. Had he been a judge, with what judicial equity and probity he would have adorned the bench. Had he been a trained musician, what glorious oratorios he might have given to the world. Had he been called to rule an empire, with what mingled ability and urbanity he would have discharged imperial functions.

But if he was not great in the eyes of men, he was great in the eyes of the Lord, and greatest because of his humility. Ordinary progress is from infancy to manhood; but, as Hudson Taylor says, Christian progress is in the reverse order, from manhood perpetually backward toward the cradle, becoming a little child again, one of God's little ones, for it is the little ones that get carried in the Father's arms and fondled.

Coleridge sagaciously hints that the highest

accompaniment of genius in the moral sphere is the carrying forward of the feelings of youth into the period of manhood and old age. Dr. Gordon more than any man I ever knew remained to the last perfectly childlike, while he put away and left behind whatever was childish.

In estimating the character of Dr. Gordon great stress should be laid on these childlike traits. The *man* of God was emphatically a *child* of God. He never lost his simplicity; he rather grew toward it than away from it; there was a perpetual return toward the spirit, attitude, and habitude of a babe in Christ. His humility and meekness, his frankness and candor, his generosity and gentleness, will always stand out conspicuous in the remembrance of all who knew him best.

The love that flooded him was, however, a supernatural grace. Seldom do we find such energy of conviction softened by such charity for differing conviction. His creed was steeped in love. He disarmed criticism by magnanimity, and blunted the weapons of controversy by the impregnable armor of an imperturbable equanimity. While I was with him on one of our missionary tours, he gave utterance to certain convictions which met strong opposition; but one of his most stubborn opponents confessed that he would rather hear Dr. Gordon when he did not agree with him than any other man when he did.

One of the most beautiful features of his work

and character was his unconsciousness of the real greatness of his attainment and achievement. When the Spirit of God controls a disciple, growth in grace and power and service becomes so natural and necessary as to be largely unconscious and in a sense involuntary. Great results come without human planning, certainly without human boasting. Mrs. Stowe said of "Uncle Tom's Cabin," that greatest work of modern fiction, that it was never begun or carried on by her with any thought of doing any great thing or becoming famous. She was simply possessed of an idea which she had to work out in a natural way, and she was a pen in the hands of God. And so yielding herself to him as an instrument, a book was produced which God used as a lever to upturn and overturn a monstrous fabric of wrong which it took a hundred years to build, and which was buttressed by commercial gains and carnal self-interest, and justified in the name of morality and even religion. A book was given to the world which Palmerston thrice read for its lessons on statesmanship, and which has been translated into fifty tongues.

This Boston pastor, even at the very last, when his successful pastorate seemed so solitary in its greatness, had no sense of having done any great thing; or if the thought of his superb triumph ever was suggested to him by others, he could only answer: "What hath God wrought!" "A man can receive nothing except it be given him from heaven."

It is true, success of such sort as his is always costly. No man ever attains such exceptional godliness, or achieves such exceptional usefulness, without getting a reputation for being eccentric, or as a fanatic, if not a heretic. Aristotle long ago said that there is no great genius without some mixture of madness; nothing supremely grand or superior was ever wrought save by a soul agitated by some great unrest and upheaved by some great purpose. The torrents that are the melting of stainless snows, high up toward heaven, and which rush down the side of the mountain to carry healing waters afar to dry and desert wastes, leave a scarred and torn mountain's breast behind. But, as Keith Falconer said: We must not fear to be thought eccentric, for what is eccentricity but being *out of center?* and we must be out of center as to the world if we would be adjusted to that other divine center of which the world knows nothing.

Such success also costs self-abnegation. The whole raising of our church-life depends on the higher standard of our ministry. "Like people, like priest." The ministry is the supreme flower and fruit of church-life—as to growth, its sign of consummation; as to fruit, its seed of propagation and reproduction. The ambition after a cultivated ministry flatters pride and carnality. But there is a culture which is fatal to the highest fruitfulness in holy things. The common wild rose has a perfectly developed seed vessel, but the double rose, the triumph of horticulture, has none—the ovaries being by cultivation absorbed into stamen and petal: the beauty of the blossom is at the expense of the fertility of the seed vessel. There is a type of ministerial scholarship that is destructively critical and proudly intellectual, and hinders soul-saving. Let it not be thought that it cost Dr. Gordon nothing to renounce and resign the proud throne among pulpit orators and biblical scholars which his gifts seemed to offer, and seek simply to be a Spirit-filled man—consenting to be misunderstood, misrepresented, ridiculed, that he might be loyal to the still small voice within his soul!

This beloved brother stands out as a *man*, a man of singularly gifted mind, with rare insight into truth and clear methods of thinking and expressing thought; a man of large and noble heart, quick in sympathy, quickened into divine love, and knowing the "expulsive power of a new affection" for Christ; a man of clean, pure tongue, whose speech was seasoned with salt and always with grace, anointed with power; a man of blameless life, in whose conduct the Babylonian conspirators would have found as little flaw as in Daniel's.

But he interests us most of all as the *man of*

God, the man of the Book, versed in the word of God; the "man in Christ" whom we have known since "fourteen years ago," who looked back for his faith to Christ's first advent, and forward for his hope to his second coming; the man of the Holy Ghost in whom the Spirit dwelt, and who dwelt in the Spirit, as the air is in us and we in it, his element; and as the man of God, of Christ, of the Spirit; in the church, a faithful preacher, loving pastor; and in the world, not of it, yet evermore to it a blessing.

Personally, the writer who pens this loving tribute never thinks of Dr. Gordon without recalling one specially memorable and delightful experience of association with him in a mission tour among the churches of Auld Scotland in 1888. After the World's Conference on Missions in Exeter Hall, London, and while we were *en route* to the "Eternal City," an invitation came from the Scottish capital, so urgent and earnest, that we should visit Edinburgh in the interest of missions before the students in the theological schools had scattered for the season, that he felt moved to abandon the Continental trip, and we went back from Paris, arriving at Edinburgh in time for a garden party at the grounds of Duncan McLaren, Esq., on Saturday afternoon, July 14. Then followed in rapid succession colossal meetings in the famous "Synod Halls" of the Free Church, and United Presbyterian body. And so great was the impression made by Dr. Gordon's knowledge of missions, grasp of the whole subject, and especially his mingled earnestness and unction, that on the sixteenth of July a crusade was proposed to be undertaken by him and the the writer jointly, among the churches of Scotland. The pressure was so great that we yielded as to the will of God, and after a week in Edinburgh, with other great meetings in the Synod Halls, we left together, visiting Oban, Inverness, Strathpeffer, Nairn, Forres, Elgin, and Aberdeen, where we spent August 5th. Dr. Gordon then felt called to return to America, and the rest of the tour was without his helpful inspiration. But wherever he went in 1888 he is remembered, and will not be forgotten while this generation lasts. That year the impulse thus given to missions was such that more candidates offered and more money was contributed than in any previous year. Would that such a man could have been spared to make a world-tour of missions and carry a like inspiration elsewhere! When we think of such a man, taken from us in his very prime, when we might have counted on twenty years more of service, we can only remember the words of Holy Scripture:

"Be still, and know that I am God."

"I was dumb with silence:"

"I opened not my mouth because Thou didst it."

"What I do thou knowest not now;"

"But thou shalt know hereafter."

We have not yet come to the point where we may penetrate the thick darkness where God dwells, and know the secrets of his purpose who doeth all things well. We can only trust blindly in the promise that all things work together for good to them that love God.

"Ye sorrow not as others which have no hope." Sorrow is not forbidden, but a hopeless sorrow is also a faithless sorrow.

We begin the New Testament with Rama, where Rachel's disconsolate grief still echoes, weeping and refusing to be comforted for those who are not. But we are to leave Rama behind as we find Him who says: "I am the Resurrection and the Life," and move on in his company toward the New Jerusalem.

Even the Psalm of Moses (90 : 15, 16) teaches us a sublime lesson in divine compensation, "Make us glad according to the days wherein thou hast afflicted us." An inspired prayer is also a prophecy. If we submit cheerfully to him he will give us gladness for every affliction and evil day, and even so great a sorrow as this shall somehow be turned into joy.

Professor Chapell has suggested a most appropriate quotation as the epitaph of this holy man and witness for Christ :

"I think it meet, as long as I am in this tabernacle,
 To stir you up by putting you in remembrance;

Knowing that shortly I must put off this my tabernacle,
Even as our Lord Jesus Christ hath shewed me.
Moreover I will endeavour that ye may be able
After my decease
To have these things always in remembrance.
For we have not followed cunningly devised fables,
When we made known unto you
The power and coming of our Lord Jesus Christ."[1]

---

[1] 2 Peter 1 : 13–16.

PART II

HOW
CHRIST CAME TO CHURCH

I

THE DREAM

NOT that I attach any importance to dreams or ever have done so. Of the hundreds which have come in the night season I cannot remember one which has proved to have had any prophetic significance either for good or ill. As a rule moreover, dreams are incongruous rather than serious, a jumble of impossible conditions in which persons and things utterly remote and unconnected are brought together in a single scene. But the one which I now describe was unlike any other within my remembrance, in that it was so orderly in its movement, so consistent in its parts, and so fitly framed together as a whole. I recognize it only as a dream; and yet I confess that the impression of it was so vivid that in spite of myself memory brings it back to me again and again, as though it were an actual occurrence in my personal history.

And yet why should it be told or deliberately committed to print? "I will come to visions and revelations of the Lord," says the apostle. His was undeniably a real, divinely given, and supernatural vision. But from the ecstasy of it, wherein he was caught up into paradise and heard unspeakable words, he immediately lets himself down to the common level of discipleship. "Yet of myself I will not glory but in my infirmities." God help us to keep to this good confession evermore; and if perchance any unusual lesson is taught even "in visions of the night when deep sleep falleth on men" let us not set ourselves up as the Lord's favorites to whom he has granted especial court privileges in the kingdom of heaven. No, the dream is not repeated as though it were a credential of peculiar saintship, or as though by it God had favored me with a supernatural revelation; but because it contains a simple and obvious lesson, out of which the entire book which we are now writing has been evolved.

It was Saturday night, when wearied from the work of preparing Sunday's sermon, that I fell asleep and the dream came. I was in the pulpit before a full congregation, just ready to begin my sermon, when a stranger entered and passed slowly up the left aisle of the church looking first to the one side and then to the other as though silently asking with his eyes that some one would give him a seat. He had proceeded nearly halfway up the aisle when a gentleman stepped out and offered him a place in his pew, which was quietly accepted. Excepting the face and features of the stranger everything in the scene is distinctly remembered—the number of the pew, the Christian man who offered its hospitality, the exact seat which was occupied. Only the countenance of the visitor could never be recalled. That his face wore a peculiarly serious look, as of one who had known some great sorrow, is clearly impressed on my mind. His bearing too was exceeding humble, his dress poor and plain, and from the beginning to the end of the service he gave the most respectful attention to the preacher. Immediately as I began my sermon my attention became riveted on this hearer. If I would avert my eyes from him for a moment they would instinctively return to him, so that he held my attention rather than I held his till the discourse was ended.

To myself I said constantly, "Who can that stranger be?" and then I mentally resolved to find out by going to him and making his acquaintance as soon as the service should be over. But after the benediction had been given the departing congregation filed into the aisles and before I could reach him the visitor had left the house. The gentleman with whom he had sat remained behind however ; and approaching him with great eagerness I asked : "Can you tell me who that stranger was who sat in your pew this morning?" In the most matter-of-course way he replied : "Why, do you not know that man? It was Jesus of Nazareth." With a sense of the keenest disappointment I said: "My dear sir, why did you let him go without introducing me to him? I was so desirous to speak with him." And with the same nonchalant air the gentleman replied: "Oh, do not be troubled. He has been here to-day, and no doubt he will come again."

And now came an indescribable rush of emotion. As when a strong current is suddenly checked, the stream rolls back upon itself and is choked in its own foam, so the intense curiosity which had been going out toward the mysterious hearer now returned upon the preacher: and the Lord himself "whose I am and whom I serve" had been listening to me to-day. What was I saying? Was I preaching on some popular theme in order to catch the ear of the public? Well, thank God it was of himself I was speaking. However imperfectly done, it was Christ and him crucified whom I was holding up this morning. But in what spirit did I preach? Was it "Christ crucified preached in a crucified style"? or did the preacher magnify himself while exalting Christ? So anxious and painful did these questionings become that I was about to ask the brother with whom he had sat if the Lord had said anything to him concerning the sermon, but a sense of propriety and self-respect at once checked the suggestion. Then immediately other questions began with equal vehemence to crowd into the mind. "What did he think of our sanctuary, its gothic arches, its stained windows, its costly and powerful organ? How was he impressed with the music and the order of the worship?" It did not seem at that moment as though I could ever again care or have the smallest curiosity as to what men might say of preaching, worship, or church, if I could only know that he had not been displeased, that he would not withhold his feet from coming again because he had been grieved at what he might have seen or heard.

We speak of "a momentous occasion." This, though in sleep, was recognized as such by the dreamer—a lifetime, almost an eternity of interest crowded into a single solemn moment. One present for an hour who could tell me all I have so longed to know; who could point out to me the imperfections of my service; who could reveal to me my real self, to whom, perhaps, I am most a stranger; who could correct the errors in our worship to which long usage and accepted tradition may have rendered us insensible. While I had been preaching for a half-hour He had been here and listening who could have told me all this and infinitely more—and my eyes had been holden that I knew him not; and now he had gone. "Yet a little while I am with you and then I go unto him that sent me."

One thought, however, lingered in my mind with something of comfort and more of awe. "*He has been here to-day, and no doubt he will come again"* ; and mentally repeating these words as one regretfully meditating on a vanished vision, "I awoke, and it was a dream." No, it was not a dream. It was a vision of the deepest reality, a miniature of an actual ministry, verifying the statement often repeated that sometimes we are most awake toward God when we are asleep toward the world.

II

HERE TO-DAY

"HERE to-day, and to come again." In this single sentence the two critical turning-points of an extended ministry are marked. It is not what we have but what we know that we have which determines our material or spiritual wealth. A poor farmer owned a piece of hard, rocky land from which, at the price of only the severest toil, he was able to support his family. He died and bequeathed his farm to his eldest son. By an accident the son discovered traces of gold on the land which, being explored, was found to contain mineral wealth of immense value. The father had had precisely the same property which the son now possessed, but while the one lived and died a poor man the other became independently rich. And yet the difference between the two depended entirely upon the fact that the son knew what he had, and the father did not know. "Where two or three are gathered in my name *there am I in the midst of them*," says Christ.

Then the dream was literally true, was it?

Yes. If this promise of the Son of God means what it says, Jesus of Nazareth was present not only on that Sunday morning, but on every Sunday morning when his disciples assemble for worship. "Why, then, oh preacher, did you not fix your attention on him from the first day you stood up in the congregation as his witness, asking how you might please him before once raising the question how you might please the people, and how in your ministry you might have his help above the help of every other? Was the dream which came to you in the transient visions of the night more real to you than his own promise, '*Lo, I am with you alway*,' which is given in that word which endureth forever?" Alas, that it was ever so! It is not what we know but what we know that we know which constitutes our spiritual wealth. I must have read and expounded these words of Jesus again and again during my ministry, but somehow for years they had no really practical meaning to me. Then came a blessed and ever-to-be-remembered crisis in my spiritual life when from a deeper insight into Scripture the doctrine of the Holy Spirit began to open to me. Now I apprehended how and in what sense Jesus is present: not in some figurative or even potential sense, but literally and really present in the Holy Spirit, his invisible self. "And I will pray the Father, and he shall give you another Comforter, that he *may abide with you for ever*" (John 14 : 16).

The coming of this other Paraclete was conditioned on the departure of Jesus: "If I go I will send him unto you." And this promise was perfectly fulfilled on Pentecost. As truly as Christ went up, the Holy Ghost came down: the one took his place at the Father's right hand in heaven, the other took his seat in the church on earth which is "builded together for a habitation of God in the Spirit." And yet, lest by this discourse about his going and the Comforter's coming we should be led to think that it is not Christ who is with us, he says, clearly referring to the Spirit: "I will not leave you orphans; *I will come to you.*" Thus it is made plain that the Lord himself is truly though invisibly here in the midst of every company of disciples gathered in any place in his name.

If Christ came to church and sat in one of the pews, what then? Would not the minister constrain him to preach to the people and allow himself to be a listener? If he were to decline and say: "I am among you as one that heareth," would he not beg him at least to give the congregation some message of his own through the lips of the preacher? If an offering for the spread of the gospel among the heathen were to be asked on that morning, would not the Master be besought to make the plea and to tell the people how he himself "though rich, for our sakes became poor that we through his poverty might be rich"? If any strife existed in the flock, would there not be an earnest appeal to him, the Good Shepherd, to guide his own sheep into the right way and to preserve the fold in peace?

Ah, yes. And Christ did come to church and abode there, but we knew it not, and therefore we took all the burden of teaching and collecting and governing on ourselves till we were often wearied with a load too heavy for us to bear. Well do we remember those days when drudgery was pushed to the point of desperation. The hearers must be moved to repentance and confession of Christ; therefore more effort must be devoted to the sermon, more hours to elaborating its periods, more pungency put into its sentences, more study bestowed on its delivery. And then came the disappointment that few, if any were converted by all this which had cost a week of solid toil. And now attention was turned to the prayer meeting as the possible seat of the difficulty —so few attending it and so little readiness to participate in its services. A pulpit scourging must be laid on next Sunday, and the sharpest sting which words can effect put into the lash. Alas, there is no increase in the attendance, and instead of spontaneity in prayer and witnessing there is a silence which seems almost like sullenness! Then the administration goes wrong and opposition is encountered among officials, so that caucusing must be undertaken to get the members to vote as they should. Thus the burdens of anxiety increase while we are trying to lighten them, and should-be helpers become hinderers, till discouragement comes and sleepless nights ensue; these hot boxes on the train of our activities necessitating a stop and a visit of the doctor, with the verdict over-work and the remedy absolute rest.

It was after much of all this of which even the most intimate friends knew nothing, that there came one day a still voice of admonition, saying, "*There standeth one among you whom ye know not.*" And perhaps I answered, "Who is he, Lord, that I might know him?" I had known the Holy Ghost as a heavenly influence to be invoked, but somehow I had not grasped the truth that he is a Person of the Godhead who came down to earth at a definite time and who has been in the church ever since, just as really as Jesus was here during the thirty and three years of his earthly life.

Precisely here was the defect. For it may be a question whose loss is the greater, his who thinks that Christ is present with him when he is not, or his who thinks not that Christ is present with him when he is? Recall the story of the missing child Jesus and how it is said that "they supposing him to be in the company went forward a day's journey." Alas, of how many nominal Christians is this true to-day! They journey on for years, saying prayers, reciting creeds, pronouncing confessions, giving alms, and doing duties, imagining all the time that because of these things Christ is with them. Happy are they if their mistake is not discovered too late for them to retrace their steps and to find, through personal regeneration, the renewed heart which constitutes the absolute essential to companionship with the Son of God.

On the other hand, how many true Christians toil on, bearing burdens and assuming responsibilities far too great for their natural strength, utterly forgetful that the mighty Burden-bearer of the world is with them to do for them and through them that which they have undertaken to accomplish alone! Happy also for these if some weary day the blessed Paraclete, the invisible Christ, shall say to them, *"Have I been so long time with you and yet hast thou not known me?"* So it happened to the writer. The strong Son of God revealed himself as being evermore in his church, and I knew him, not through a sudden burst of revelation, not through some thrilling experience of instantaneous sanctification, but by a quiet, sure, and steady discovery, increasing unto more and more. Jesus in the Spirit stood with me in a kind of spiritual epiphany and just as definitely and irrevocably as I once took Christ crucified as my sin-bearer I now took the Holy Spirit for my burden-bearer.

"Then you received the baptism of the Holy Spirit did you?" some one will ask. Well, we prefer not to use an expression which is not strictly biblical. The great promise, "Ye shall be baptized in the Holy Ghost" was fulfilled on the day of Pentecost once for all, as it seems to us. Then the Paraclete was given for the entire dispensation, and the whole church present and future was brought into the economy of the Spirit, as it is written : "For in one Spirit were we all baptized into one body" (1 Cor. 12 : 13, R. V.). But for God to give is one thing ; for us to receive is quite another. "God so loved that he gave his only begotten Son," is the word of our Lord to Nicodemus. But it is written also: "As many as *received* him to them gave he power to become the sons of God." In order to regeneration and sonship it is as absolutely essential for us to receive as for God to have given. So on the day of Pentecost the Holy Spirit, as the Comforter, Advocate, Helper, and Teacher and Guide, was given to the church. The disciples who before had been regenerated by the Spirit, as is commonly held, now received the Holy Ghost to qualify and empower them for service. It was another and higher experience than that which they had hitherto known. It is the difference between the Holy Spirit for renewal and the Holy Spirit for ministry. Even Jesus, begotten by the Holy Ghost and therefore called "the Son of God," did not enter upon his public service till he had been "anointed," or "sealed," with that same

Spirit through whom he had been begotten. So of his immediate apostles ; so of Paul, who had been converted on the way to Damascus. So of the others mentioned in the Acts, as the Samaritan Christians and the Ephesian disciples (19 : 1–8). And not a few thoughtful students of Scripture maintain that the same order still holds good ; that there is such a thing as receiving the Holy Ghost in order to qualification for service. It is not denied that many may have this blessing in immediate connection with their conversion, from which it need not necessarily be separated. Only let it be marked that as the giving of the Spirit by the Father is plainly spoken of, so distinctly is the receiving of the Spirit on the part of the disciples constantly named in Scripture. When the risen Christ breathed on his disciples and said : "Receive ye the Holy Ghost," it is an active not a passive reception which is pointed out, as in the invitation : "Whosoever will, let him take the water of life freely." Here the same word is used as also in the Epistle to the Galatians. "Received ye the Spirit by the works of the law, or by the hearing of faith ?" (3 : 2).

God forbid that we should lay claim to any higher attainment than the humblest. We are simply trying to answer, as best we may from Scripture, the question asked above about the baptism of the Holy Ghost. On the whole, and after prolonged study of the Scripture, we cannot resist this conviction : As Christ, the second person of the Godhead, came to earth to make atonement for sin and to give eternal life, and as sinners we must receive him by faith in order to forgiveness and sonship, so the Holy Spirit, the third person of the Godhead, came to the earth to communicate the "power from on high"; and we must as believers in like manner receive him by faith in order to be qualified for service. Both gifts have been bestowed, but it is not what we have but what we know that we have by a conscious appropriating faith, which determines our spiritual wealth. Why then should we be satisfied with "the forgiveness of sins, according to the riches of his grace" (Eph. 1 : 7), when the Lord would grant us also "according to the riches of his glory, to be strenghened with might by his Spirit in the inner man"? (Eph. 3 : 16.)

To return to personal experience. I am glad that one of the most conservative as well as eminent theological professors of our times, has put this matter exactly as I should desire to see it stated. He says: "If a reference to personal experience may be permitted, I may indeed here set my seal. Never shall I forget the gain to conscious faith and peace which came to my own soul not long after the first decisive and appropriating view of the crucified Lord as the sinner's sacrifice of peace, from a more intelligent and conscious hold upon the living and most gracious personality of the Holy Spirit through whose mercy the soul had got that view. It was a new development of insight into the love of God. It was a new contact, as it were, with the inner and eternal movements of redeeming love and power, and a new discovery in divine resources. At such a time of finding gratitude and love and adoration we gain a new, a newly realized reason and motive power and rest." [1]

" A conscious hold upon the personality of the Holy Spirit ; " "a newly realized motive power." Such it was ; not the sending down of some new power from heaven in answer to long waiting and prayer, but an " articulating into " a power already here, but hitherto imperfectly known and appropriated. Just in front of the study window where I write is a street, above which it is said that a powerful electric current is constantly moving. I cannot see that current: it does not report itself to hearing, or sight, or taste, or smell, and so far as the testimony of the senses is to be taken, I might reasonably discredit its existence. But I see a slender arm, called the trolley, reaching up and touching it ; and immediately the car with its heavy load of passengers moves along the track as though seized in the grasp of some mighty giant. The power had been there before, only now the car lays hold of it or is rather laid hold

---

[1] Principal H. C. G. Moule, Ridley Hall, Cambridge, Eng., "*Veni Creator Spiritus,*" p. 13.

of by it, since it was a touch, not a grip, through which the motion was communicated. And would it be presumptuous for one to say that he had known something of a similar contact with not merely a divine force but a divine person? The change which ensued may be described thus: Instead of praying constantly for the descent of a divine influence there was now a surrender, however imperfect, to a divine and ever-present Being: instead of a constant effort to make use of the Holy Spirit for doing my work there arose a clear and abiding conviction that the true secret of service lay in so yielding to the Holy Spirit that he might use me to do his work. Would that the ideal might be so perfectly realized that over whatever remains of an earthly ministry, be it shorter or longer, might be written the slightly changed motto of Adolphe Monod:

"All through Christ: in the Holy Spirit: for the glory of God. All else is nothing."

III

AND TO COME AGAIN

THE apprehension of the doctrine of Christ's second advent came earlier than the realization of the other doctrine, that of his abiding presence in the church in the Holy Spirit. But its discovery constituted a no less distinct crisis in my ministry. "This same Jesus, which is taken up from you into heaven, *shall so come in like manner as ye have seen him go into heaven*," is the parting promise of Jesus to his disciples, communicated through the two men in white apparel, as a cloud received him out of their sight. When after more than fifty years in glory he breaks the silence and speaks once more in the Revelation which he gave to his servant John, the post-ascension Gospel which he sends opens with, "*Behold, he cometh with clouds*," and closes with "*Surely I come quickly*." Considering the solemn emphasis thus laid upon this doctrine, and considering the great prominence given to it throughout the teaching of our Lord and of his apostles, how was it that for the first five years of my pastoral life it had absolutely no place in my preaching? Undoubtedly the reason lay in the lack of early instruction. Of all the sermons heard from childhood on, I do not remember listening to a single one upon this subject. In the theological course, while this truth had its place indeed, it was taught as in most theological seminaries of this country, according to the post-millennial interpretation; and with the most reverent respect for the teachers holding this view I must express my mature conviction that, though the doctrine of our Lord's second coming is not ignored in this system, it is placed in such a setting as to render it quite impractical as a theme for preaching and quite inoperative as a motive for Christian living. For if a millennium must intervene before the return of our Lord from heaven, or if the world's conversion must be accomplished before he shall come in his glory, how is it possible for his disciples in this present time to obey his words: "Watch, therefore, for ye know not what hour your Lord shall come"?

I well remember in my early ministry hearing two humble and consecrated laymen speaking of this hope in the meetings of the church, and urging it upon Christians as the ground of unworldliness and watchfulness of life. Discussion followed with these good brethren, and then a searching of the Scriptures to see if these things were so; and then a conviction of their truth; and then? The godly William Hewitson declares that the discovery of the scriptural hope of our Lord's second coming wrought in him a change amounting almost to a second conversion. What if another, not presuming to be named in company with this consecrated saint, should nevertheless set his hand and seal to the affirmation that the strongest and most permanent impulse of his ministry came from his apprehension of the blessed hope of our Lord's second coming?

But how is it that this doctrine, so plainly and conspicuously written in Scripture, could have remained so long undiscovered? In answering this question we see how little ground we have for glorying over the Jews. They did not recognize Christ in his first advent because they discerned in Scripture only those predictions which announced him as a reigning and conquering Messiah. This conception they wove into a veil of exposition and tradition so thick that when Jesus appeared as the lowly and humble Nazarene they knew him not, but "hid as it were their faces from him." And this strong prepossession still obscures their vision so that "even unto this day when Moses is read the veil is upon their heart."

With the larger mass of Gentile Christians the case is just the reverse. They know Christ crucified, and believing that the Cross is to conquer the world and that the preaching of the gospel in the present dispensation is to bring all men to God, they see no need of the personal coming of the Christ as king to subdue all things under his feet and to reign visibly on the earth. This conception in turn has been woven into an elaborate veil of tradition for Gentile believers and "until this day, remaineth the same veil untaken away" in the reading of the New Testament.

It was not so in the beginning. For three hundred years the church occupied the position of a bride awaiting the return of the bridegroom from heaven—she, meantime, holding herself free from all alliance with this world, content to fulfill her calling in witnessing for Christ, in suffering with Christ, and so to accomplish her appointed work of the gathering out of the elect body for the Lord "until he come." A strange and almost grotesque conception to many modern Christians no doubt. But it was while maintaining this attitude that the church moved on most rapidly and irresistibly in her missionary conquests.

Then came the foreshadowings of the great apostasy. The world which had been a foe to the church became her friend and patron; Constantine, the emperor of Rome, became her head, and thus the eyes of Christians began to be withdrawn from him who is "Head over all things to his church." The great and good Augustine yielded to the seduction and was among the first to teach that in the temporal triumph of Christianity the kingdom had already come, though the

King with whose return the primitive church had been wont to identify the appearing of the kingdom was still absent. Little by little, as the apostasy deepened, this early hope of Christians became eclipsed till, in the words of Auberlin, "when the church became a harlot she ceased to be a bride who goes forth to meet her Bridegroom," and thus chiliasm disappeared. What moreover would have been deemed an apostasy in the primitive church grew into a tradition and a creed in the post-Nicene church, which creed until this day largely rules the faith of Christians.

Within fifty years, however, there has been a widespread revival of the early teaching on this point, especially among the most eminent evangelists and missionary promoters, until to-day in a great company of devout Christians, the uplifted gaze is once more visible, and the advent cry "Even so come, Lord Jesus," is once more heard.

"But tell me," we hear some one saying, "how it is that this doctrine can have such an inspiring and uplifting influence as you claim for it?" We answer, in more ways than can be described in a single chapter.

"The doctrine of the Lord's second coming as it appears in the New Testament," says an eminent Scotch preacher, "is like a lofty mountain which dominates the entire landscape." An admirable illustration! For in such a case, no matter what road you take, no matter what pass you tread, you will find the mountain bursting on your vision at every turn of the way and at every parting of the hills. What first struck me now, in reading the New Testament, was something like this : Whatever doctrine I was pursuing, whatever precept I was enforcing, I found it fronting toward and terminating in the hope of the Lord's second coming. Is watchfulness amid the allurements of the world enjoined, the exhortation is : "Watch therefore ; *for ye know not what hour your Lord doth come*" (Matt. 24 : 42). Is patience under trial and injustice counseled ? The word is : "Be patient therefore, brethren, *unto the coming of the Lord*" (James 5 : 7). Is an ideal church presented concerning whose deportment the apostle "needs not to speak anything" ? Its commendation is : "Ye turned to God from idols to serve the living and true God ; and *to wait for his Son from heaven*" (1 Thess. 1 : 9, 10). Is holy living urged ? This is the inspiring motive thereto : "That, denying ungodliness and worldly lusts, we should live soberly, righteously, and godly, in this present world ; *looking for that blessed hope, and the glorious appearing of the great God and our Saviour Jesus Christ*" (Titus 2 : 12, 13). All paths of obedience and service lead onward to the mountain. Our command to service bids us "Occupy *till I come*" (Luke 19 : 13). In observing the Lord's Supper we "shew the Lord's death *till he come*" (1 Cor. 11 : 26). In the injunction to fidelity the word is that we "keep this commandment without spot, unrebukable, *until the appearing of our Lord Jesus Christ*" (1 Tim. 6 : 14). Let any candid reader collate the texts in the New Testament on this subject, and he will see that our statement as to the pre-eminence of this doctrine is not exaggerated.

To pursue the figure farther. As all the roads lead toward the mountain, so conversely the mountain looks out upon all the roads. Take your stand in the doctrine of the Lord's coming and make it your point of observation for viewing Scripture, and your map of redemption will very soon take shape, and the relation of part to part will become apparent. Just as Christ crucified is the center of soteriology, so Christ coming again is the center of eschatology. Place the Saviour where the Scriptures place him, on the cross— "who his own self bare our sins in his own body on the tree"—and all the teachings of the ceremonial law become intelligible, and its types and offerings fit together into one harmonious system. God forbid that we should by a grain's weight lesson the emphasis upon Christ crucified. This is the central fact of redemption accomplished. Even so put Christ coming into his scriptural place and all the prophecies and Messianic hopes of the Old Testament and the New become intelligible— the establishment of the kingdom, the restoration of Israel, the renewing of all things. These two centers—Christ crucified and Christ coming—must be rigidly maintained if all the Bible is to be utilized and all its teachings harmonized.

So the writer bears joyful testimony that the discovery of this primitive doctrine of the gospel, the personal pre-millennial coming of Christ, constituted a new era in his study of the word of God, and gave an opening-out into vistas of truth hitherto undreamed of. And moreover, apart from the question of eschatology, it was the means of the deepest and firmest anchoring in all the doctrines of the evangelical faith. Why should not this be the case? If it is true, as one has said, that "when the smallest doctrine in the body of truth is mutilated it is sure to avenge itself upon the whole system," why should it not be even more certainly the case, that one of the mountain truths of Scripture being recognized, all neighboring doctrines should be lifted into distincter prominence around its base? At all events, I confess myself so indebted to this hope in every way, that I cannot measure the loss it would have been to have passed through a ministry of twenty-five years without knowledge of it.

And as to the relation of this truth to Christian life : Is not an unworldly and single-eyed ministry the supreme need in these days of a materialized civilization and a secularized church? And where shall the most powerful motive to such a ministry be found? No one who reads the New Testament carefully can deny that our Lord has lodged it in the hope of his second coming. We may not see how the doctrine should have that effect; but if he has so ordained, it will certainly be found true in actual experience. I recall a lecture which I heard some years since from a scholarly preacher in which he aimed to show that Christ's second coming so far from being personal and literal is a spiritual and perpetual fact; that he is coming all the time in civilization, in the diffusion of Christianity, and in the march of human progress. He closed his argument by questioning seriously what practical influence upon Christian life the anticipation of an event so mysterious and so uncertain as to time and circumstance can have. Being asked to speak, I related a little household incident which had recently occurred. Having gone into the country with my children for a few weeks' vacation, I had planned with them many pleasant diversions and engagements for the holidays, when almost upon my arrival I was summoned back to the city on an important mission. In the disappointment of the children I said to them: "Children, I am going to the city to-day. But I shall soon be back again. I may come to-morrow, or the next day, or the day after, or possibly not till the end of the week, but you may expect me any time." It so happened that I was detained until Saturday. But when I returned I learned that in their eagerness to welcome me back the children, contrary to their natural instincts, had insisted on having their faces washed every day and upon having on their clean clothes and going down to meet me at train time. "A good story," exclaimed the lecturer, "but it is not an argument." Ah, but is it not? Human life is often found to be the best expositor of Scripture. He who put his sublimest doctrines into parables drawn from common experience can often be best understood through some homely household incident. He would have his servants always washed, and clothed in white raiment during his absence. If we believe that he will not return till hundreds of years have elapsed, we may reasonably delay our purification and make no haste to put on our white raiment. But what if his coming is ever imminent? Let this truth be deeply realized and let the parables in which he affirms it become household words to us, and who shall say that it will be without effect? One at least may with all humility testify to its influence in shaping his ministry. Without imparting any sombre hue to Christian life; without "replacing glory with gloom" in the heart which should rejoice evermore, it is enough to say that when "the solemn *Maranatha*" resounds constantly through the soul, the most powerful impulse is awakened toward our doing with all diligence what he would have us do, and our being with all the heart what he would have us be.

"Then your dream came true, did it?" No; rather it had been true before it was dreamed, and the vision was a kind of *résumé* of a quarter-century ministry. *Here now in the Holy Spirit and to come again in person!* These were two discoveries which, added to the fundamental truths already realized, brought unspeakable blessing into one Christian experience. We reiterate emphatically that that night-vision has never been regarded as anything supernatural or extraordinary in itself. Nevertheless there it stands to-day in the hall of memory, a dream-parable as clean-cut and distinctly outlined as a marble statue, with the legend inwrought in it, "*Here to-day and to come to-morrow,*" so that in spite of knowledge to the contrary it comes back again and again as an occurrence of actual history. Call it a dream of mysticism? What if rather it might be named a vision of primitivism? The most eminent living master of ecclesiastical history, Harnack, photographing in a single sentence the church of the earliest centuries, says: "*Originally the church was the heavenly Bride of Christ, the abiding place of the Holy Spirit.*" Does the reader not see that here is the same twofold conception—Christ in-resident in the church by the Spirit; and Christ expected to return in person as the Bridegroom for his bride? This was the church which moved with such rapid and triumphant progress against ancient heathenism. With no power except "the irresistible might of weakness"; with no wealth except the riches of glory inherited through her heavenly citizenship; refusing all compromise with the world, declining all patronage of kings and emperors, she nevertheless went forth conquering and to conquer, till in a few years she had undermined the whole colossal fabric of paganism. And might not the church of Christ do the same to-day if she were to return to this primitive ideal? and if renouncing her dependence on human resources—wealth and power and social prestige, she were to inscribe upon her banner that ancient motto: "Not by might nor by power, but by my Spirit, saith the Lord." Such is the train of questioning started by a dream.

IV

IF I HAD NOT COME

TO see Christ is to see ourselves by startling contrast. The religious leaders of our Saviour's day were sinners before they knew him, but their sin was not manifested. "If I had not come and spoken unto them they had not had sin," said Jesus, "but now they have no cloak for their sin." The Son of God is *Christus Revelator* before he is *Christus Salvator*. No truer testimony to the Messiahship was ever uttered than that of the Samaritan woman: "Come and see a man that told me all things that ever I did. Is not this the Christ?"

If Christ came to church it were a sacred privilege to entertain him; and evermore the aisles which he had trodden would be counted holy ground. But are we ready for the revelations which his coming is sure to bring? His glory would certainly manifest our guilt. Ah, yes! And his lowly garb would also rebuke our costly attire, and his deep humility would shame the diamonds on jeweled Christian fingers. Does the reader remember how, in the dream, I saw him looking first to the one side and then to the other, as he walked up the aisle on that Sunday morning, as though silently begging for a seat? Well, though there had been misgivings and questionings about our system of pew rentals, with the sittings so graded that one could read the relative financial standing of the worshipers by noting their position in the broad aisles, the matter had not come home to me as a really serious question till Christ came to church on that morning. Judging by his dress and bearing it was evident that were he to become a regular attendant, he could not afford the best pew in the house : and this was distressing to think of, since I knew from Scripture that he has long since been accorded the highest place in heaven, "angels and authorities and powers being made subject unto him." And there were other things in our worship whose presence caused great searchings of heart, so soon as the Master of assemblies was recognized as being there.

To translate the dream into plain literal prose: When it became a realized and unquestionable fact that, in the person of the Holy Ghost, Jesus is just as truly in the midst of the church as he once stood in the company of his disciples and "showed them his hands and his feet," then the whole house began to be searched as with a lifted candle. Yes! And he is among us no longer "as one that serveth" but as "a Son over his own house, whose house are we if we hold fast the confidence and the rejoicing of the hope firm unto the end." We who worship and we who conduct worship are simply his servants to do only what he bids us do, and to speak and act by the guidance of his Spirit.

And judgment began with the pulpit as that mysterious man in yonder pew looked toward it and listened, though he spoke not a word. The theme had been scriptural and evangelical, as we have already said: but with what spirit was it presented? We have "preached the gospel unto you *in the Holy Ghost sent forth from heaven*" (1 Peter 1 : 12, R. V.), is almost the only homiletical direction found in Scripture. And yet how deep and searching the words! We are not to use the Holy Spirit in preaching: he is to use us. As the wind pours through the organ pipes, causing their voice to be heard, albeit according to the distinctive tone and pitch of each, so the Spirit speaks through each minister of Christ according to his special gift, that the people may hear the word of the Lord. Is it not the most subtle temptation which comes to the preacher that he allow himself to be played upon by some other spirit than the Paraclete? the popular desire for eloquence, for humor, for entertainment, for wit, and originality, moving him before he is aware, to speak for the applause of men rather than for the approval of Christ? Not until the presence in the assembly of the Spirit of the Lord is recognized does this error come painfully home to the conscience. We must not enter into personal experience here, further than to tell the reader how repeatedly we have turned to the following paragraph in the Journal of John Woolman, the Quaker, and read and re-read it :

"One day, being under a strong exercise of spirit, I stood up and said some words in meeting, but not keeping close to the divine opening, I said more than was required of me. Being soon sensible of my error, I was afflicted in mind some weeks, without any light or comfort even to that degree that I could not take satisfaction in anything. I remembered God and was troubled, and in the depth of my distress he had pity on me, and sent the Comforter. . . . Being thus humbled and disciplined under the cross, *my understanding became more strengthened to distinguish the pure Spirit which moves inwardly upon the heart*, and which taught me to wait in silence, sometimes many weeks together, until I felt that rise which prepares the creature to stand like a trumpet through which the Lord speaks to his flock."

Here is a bit of heart biography so antique and strange to that spirit of unrestrained utterance which characterizes our time, that it almost needs an interpreter to make it intelligible ; but if one has ever considered deeply the requirement to speak in the Spirit, its meaning will be very plain. Is it not as true of our spirits as of our bodies that the severest colds which we contract come to us from sitting in a draught? Perhaps a current of popular applause strikes us and before we know it our fervor has become chilled, and then we find ourselves preaching self instead of preaching Christ, giving more heed to rhetorical effect than to spiritual impression, till the Lord mercifully humbles us and shows us our sin. Well were it if we could sometimes impose on ourselves the penance of "silence many weeks together" till we should learn to "keep close to the divine opening."

What was it then that Jesus in the Spirit seemed to demand as he appeared in church that morning? What but the freedom of the place accorded to him who built the house and therefore "hath more honor than the house"? Is it not written that "where the Spirit of the Lord is, there is liberty"? Not liberty for us to do as we will surely, but liberty for him to do as he will. And where is the Spirit now but in the church, his only sanctuary in this dispensation? Let there be no restrictions on his house then, lest—if in his revelation the Spirit shall,

> Show us that loving man
> That rules the courts of bliss,

coming into our assembly to-day "poor and in vile raiment"—he shall hear the word: "Stand thou there or sit here under my footstool ;" while to the "man with a gold ring and goodly apparel" the invitation is given : "Sit thou here in a good place."

And the Spirit must have equal liberty in the pulpit, so that if he choose to come into the sermon in the garb of plain and homely speech, he may not be refused a hearing. Indeed, it was just this accusation that came to one unveiled heart as Christ showed himself in yonder pew—the conviction that he might have been fenced out of the sermon many times when he had desired to be heard therein, because the discourse had been so elaborately pre-arranged and so exactly written out that after-thoughts were excluded though they should come direct from him.

Ah, yes; and that was not the deepest revelation. If Christ is present in the pulpit he must think his thoughts through us as well as speak his words by our lips. And what if these thoughts, like their Master, should be to some hearers like "a root out of a dry ground," having no beauty that they should desire them? Art thou ready, oh preacher, to take all the consequences of letting the Lord speak through thee as he will? This may sometimes lead thee out of the beaten path of accepted opinion and into ways that seem devious to sacred tradition. And this in turn, though done in humility, may bring upon thee the accusation of pride of opinion as though thou wert saying : "I have more understanding than all my teachers." Does the reader know the story of John Tauler, the mystic, and of that anointing and illumination of the Spirit which came to him after he had been for several years an eloquent preacher? He represents some former teacher as chiding him for departing from his instructions; to which he replies : "But if the highest Teacher of all truth come to a man he must be empty and quit of all else and hear his voice only. Know ye that when this same Master cometh to me he teaches me more in one hour than you and all the doctors from Adam down." Bold words! Let us reverence our teachers and seek to know how much the Lord hath taught us through them; let the words of commentators, who have prayed and pored over God's holy word to search out precious ore for us, be honored for all the wealth that they have brought to us, knowing that only "*with all saints*," can we "comprehend what is the breadth and length and depth and height" of the love of Christ which passeth knowledge. Nevertheless, it is good sometimes with Tauler "to be empty and quit of all else and hear his voice only." And that it might be so is perhaps the reason why Christ came to church that day. The world is full of books which demand our study if we would know the mysteries of God; criticism has set up its "scientific method," declaring that what in the Bible cannot stand the test must be discarded. But while the vendors of learning are crying "Lo here," and "Lo there," the Good Shepherd speaks, saying : "My sheep hear my voice"; and he is still in the fold to care for his own, to lead them into green pastures where the freshest and sweetest truth is found ; to make them lie down by still waters in which they may see his own blessed face reflected. Only let not the sheep hear the voice of strangers who know not the truth : let them hear only Christ.

He is not present in the church by his Spirit as critic and censor of the preacher, but as his gracious helper and counselor. Then give him liberty of utterance in your sermon, oh, man of God! All our acquirements in knowledge of the world, all our mastery of style and expression he will use, if it is surrendered to him. But this is not enough. There must be such a line of Scripture exposition in the sermon that the Spirit shall have free course to "ride triumphantly through it in his own chariot," the inspired word ; and there must be in it such windows looking toward "the divine opening" that he may find entrance at every point with suggestions, illuminations, inspirations. Let those who know bear witness whether, when preaching in such a frame, thoughts have not come in, far better than any which we had premeditated, lessons, illustrations, and admonitions fitted to the occasion and to the hearer as we could never have fitted them of ourselves. "So after many mortifications and failures when going to this warfare at mine own charges," writes one, "I found that on this day I had been at ease and had had liberty in prophesying, and withal had spoken better than I knew, and I said: 'Surely the Lord is in this place and I knew it not.'"

> Give me to see thee and to feel
>   The mutual vision clear;
> The things unseen reveal, reveal,
>   And let me know them near.

V

IN THY LIGHT

WITHIN the church of God the quality of actions depends not altogether upon what they are in themselves, but what they are in their relation to Christ. Many things, quite innocent in their proper sphere, become profane when brought into that temple where God, the Holy Ghost, has his dwelling place.

That mysterious stranger who awed me by his presence in church on that morning, is no ascetic. It cannot be forgotten that he once mingled in the festivities of a marriage feast in Cana, and that he drew about him sportive children and took them in his arms and blessed them. "And if Christ is such a one, oh preacher! do not make his church a mournful place where we must repress all exhibitions of natural joy and social good cheer, and become as the hypocrites are who disfigure their faces that they may appear unto men to fast." Well-spoken counsel, no doubt! Yet Christ is still Christ; and he has never outgrown the print of the nails. So confident of this am I that in dreaming over my dream in waking hours, it always seemed certain to me that, had I come near to him on that memorable Sabbath morning, I should have discerned the marks of his crucifixion in his body. What John the apostle is represented as saying of our Lord still holds true:

> Cheerful he was to us:
> But let me tell you, sons, he was within
> A pensive man, and always had a load
> Upon his spirits.

A convivial Christ is not quite the personage that rises up before us in the prophets and in the Gospels. And yet when one observes the pleasant devices for introducing men to him, which abound in the modern church—the music, the feasts, the festivals, and the entertainments— it would seem as though this were a very prevalent conception. No! Jesus is the serious Christ, the faithful and true witness who will never cover up his scars in order to win disciples. Our latter day Christianity would not abolish the cross indeed, but it seeks so to festoon it with flowers, that the offense thereof may be hidden out of sight. If Christ crucified is "unto the Greeks foolishness," why not first present him in some other character if any of this cultured people are among the hearers? But does not the reader remember that when "certain Greeks" came to worship at the feast, saying "we would see Jesus," the first recorded word which the Saviour spoke to them was: "Verily, verily, I say unto you, Except a corn of wheat fall into the ground and die it abideth alone ; but if it die it bringeth forth much fruit," thus presenting the whole deep doctrine of the cross in a single condensed parable ? Never has there been such a laborious attempt to popularize Christ as in the closing years of this nineteenth century. But if the Saviour were to come to church and reveal himself to those who have so mistaken his identity, we can well think of his saying : " Behold my hands and my feet *that it is I myself;* handle me and see." Ah, yes ! here are the tokens by which we recognize his real personality. "I perceive that Christ suffered only his wounds to be touched after he had risen from the dead," says Pascal, " as though he would teach us that henceforth we can be united to him only through his sufferings."

But it is Christ in the Spirit not Christ in the flesh whom we recognize as dwelling in the church now ; and it is the church as a spiritual temple builded of living stones, not a material structure fashioned of wood or granite and consecrated to the Lord of which we are now speaking. Yes, and out of this conception came the heartsearching and the house-searching of which we write.

I have told the reader how having in vision recognized Christ as present on that morning, an intense anxiety seized me as to whether everything in the ordering of his house was as he would have it.

There was a choir in yonder gallery, employed at an expense of nearly three thousand dollars, to sing the praises of God in his church. Some of the number were believers; the larger part made no profession of discipleship, and some were confessed disbelievers. But they had fine voices, therefore were they there. No word of criticism can be passed upon them, since they were serving solely by the appointment of the church. But when now the presence of Christ by the Holy Ghost was realized, the minister of the flock began to have pangs of indescribable misgiving about this way of administering the service of song. Had it not been a method long in vogue? Yes. And did it not conform to the general usage of Christian congregations? Yes. Then why have scruples about it? There might have been none but for the presence of that revered man from heaven. But Christ has come to church : "and who may abide the day of his coming? and who shall stand when he appeareth? for he is like a refiner's fire and like fuller's soap." And the burning of that fire began from that day, and could never thenceforth be quenched : and the cleansing must now go on to the end.

Does the Scripture deal in poetry or in fact when it says to the church, the body of believers : "Know ye not that ye are the temple of God and that the Spirit of God dwelleth in you?" Into the inner court of that Jewish temple went the high priest alone, once every year, "not *without blood.*" Not the less rigidly was it required of the common priests who "went into the first tabernacle, accomplishing the service of God," that they should come first to the brazen altar of sacrifice and then to the laver of cleansing in order to be qualified for their ministry. And these things happened for ensamples unto us. The types are as rigid and unchangeable in their teaching as mathematics. The altar and the laver; the blood and the water: our justification by the cross and our sanctification by the Spirit—these two are absolutely prerequisite and their order is forever fixed. David under the old covenant sought for the true qualification of an acceptable worshiper when he prayed: "*Purge me with hyssop and I shall be clean; wash me and I shall be whiter than snow.*" It was first the blood and then the water. The exhortation to the worshiper under the new covenant is precisely the same: " Let us draw near, . . . having our hearts sprinkled from an evil conscience and having our bodies *washed with pure water*" (Heb. 10 : 22). First cleansing by the blood, then sanctification by the Spirit.

The congregation of the regenerate church now constitutes the earthly priesthood under Christ our great High Priest. He could not enter into the holiest in heaven except by his own blood; no more can any one on earth perform the smallest service in the worship of his house—that "holy temple in the Lord, builded together for a habitation of God through the Spirit"—who has not been justified by the blood of Christ. This was the deep and abiding conviction which seized one minister of Christ as his eyes were opened by the coming of the Lord to search his sanctuary. And then followed unutterable distress of conscience about this whole grave question. There were those singers standing above the communion table, leading a divinely appointed ministry of song. And yet the question had never been asked whether they had come under the cleansing of the blood of Christ and the renewing of the Holy Spirit; only whether they had fine voices, well trained and harmonious. The situation brought such burden of soul that sometimes the whole service—the prayer, the praise, the sermon—was gone through with under indescribable constraint and spiritual repression. When the mind of Christ was sought for in the matter, his voice was heard saying: "God is a Spirit, and they that worship him *must worship in spirit and in truth*." Half the stanzas sung in an ordinary service are such that unconverted persons could not possibly sing them in truth, and none of them could they sing in "the Spirit." Then came the habit of searching for hymns more neutral and more remote from Christian experience, lest I should be the occasion of causing any to speak falsely in God's presence. And more than all, came what may be called a corporate conviction, a taking of blame on behalf of the whole church concerning this matter. For plainly the sin seemed nothing else than simony. The Lord has appointed the Holy Ghost to be the inspirer and director of sacred song in his temple : "Be filled with the Spirit, speaking one to another in psalms and hymns and spiritual songs, singing and making melody with your heart to the Lord" (Eph. 5 : 18, 19, R. V.). This delight of sacred song is greatly coveted ; and they who have wealth say, "We will give you three thousand dollars that you may buy this gift of the Holy Ghost, and may bring in singing men and singing women, the best that can be procured, that the attractions of our sanctuary may not be a whit behind the chiefest in all the city." And it seemed to me that the voice of the Spirit concerning it all would be : "Thy money perish with thee, because thou hast thought that the gift of God may be purchased with money."

Then in thought the vision came back, and yonder silent Christ seemed to speak : "Reach hither thy finger and behold my hands ; and reach hither thy hand and thrust it into my side." And while we wondered he reasoned with us saying : "Who think ye that I am, oh, my brethren ? And wherefore came I unto that hour when my soul was exceeding sorrowful, even unto death?" Was it that you might live delicately and bring in the minstrels to perform before you in my house? Behold they that live delicately are in king's courts; but ye are they whom I have appointed to bear the cross and to fill up that which is behind of the afflictions of Christ for his body's sake, which is the church. "*The sacrifice of praise, even the fruit of the lips,*" have I enjoined upon you; but the luxury of sumptuous music, who has required it at your hands? Wherefore do ye spend your money for that which is not bread, when millions are perishing for the bread of life which I have commanded you to bring them; and I still wait to see of the travail of my soul and be satisfied?

As I heard all this the whole heart became sick. I thought of churches which were bestowing ten times, and in some instances fifty times as much for artistic music as they contributed to foreign missions, and I said: "We are believers by the cleansing of the blood and by the indwelling of the Spirit; have been constituted '*a spiritual house, an holy priesthood to offer up spiritual sacrifices*'; but instead of using our ministry in humble dependence on the Holy Ghost, we have brought up minstrels from Egypt, that 'music with its voluptuous swell' may take the place of that chastened, self-denying, holy song which no man can learn but they that have been redeemed."

And out of this storm of questioning and misgiving, and all this deep inquisition of conscience, there arose at last one of the calmest, maturest, and most unconquerable convictions of my life. I could never in any circumstance accept a ministry where the worship appointed by God has been so perverted by men. Not in the language of metaphor or of poetry, but in the words of literal truth I hear God saying : *"For the temple of God is holy, which temple ye are."* When I can consent to have the communion table moved out into the court of the Gentiles, and call upon the thoughtless and unconverted to receive the sacred elements lying thereon, then I may see the propriety of bringing a choir of unregenerated musical artists into the Holy of Holies of the church, and of committing to their direction the service of song. This conviction rests neither upon prejudice nor preference, but upon the fixed assurance that in the house of God I am servant, not the master, and that I have no alternative but to comply strictly with the divine arrangements of the church fixed by the Lord himself.

When I had written all this I imagined I heard some reader exclaiming : "Is not this a Pharisee of the Pharisees risen up within the Christian church, and tithing the mint, anise and cummin of religious worship? Is there really any ground for his scruples, or anything practical in his suggestions?" Let this appear in later chapters.

VI

THE TEMPLE OF GOD IS HOLY

RECALL a sermon by President Wayland, preached while I was a student, in which he spoke thus, in brief, about amusements: "You ask me if it is sinful for Christians to play cards. Well, you remember that the Roman soldiers threw dice and cast lots while our Saviour was dying on the cross. But you as his disciples, had you been present, could not have taken part in that game of chance. And why should you do so now before whose eyes Jesus Christ hath been evidently set forth crucified among you?"

It was a practical and pointed way of setting forth a great principle. The church, which has journeyed on for nearly nineteen hundred years, has never left the crucified Christ behind. I make no reference here to a material sanctuary with the cross and passion,—symbols wrought into its ecclesiastical architecture,—but to that "holy temple in the Lord" in which we are "builded together for a habitation of God through the Spirit." It is in this house that we stand during the entire discussion. As we mark on every hand its divine architecture, we observe that the cross is inwrought with each article of its furniture. In the ordinance through which we enter the temple, we are *"baptized into his death."* In the communion which we keep perpetually within its courts, we *" do show the Lord's death till he come."* In the pulpit where the gospel is proclaimed, *" we preach Christ crucified*, the power of God and the wisdom of God." In the songs which we sing we offer *" the sacrifice of praise* to God continually, that is the fruit of our lips." Thus the crucified One is visible in every service and sacrament of his temple. That solemn stranger in yonder pew did not " cry nor lift up nor cause his voice to be heard " in his temple ; for in each act of worship he had ordained that his word should be heard, saying : " I am he that liveth *and was dead*, and behold I am alive for evermore."

Once standing within this holy temple of the church a great apostle wept because " the enemies of the cross of Christ " had come in thither (Phil. 3 : 18, 19). Who were they ? Heretics, who had denied the atonement and effaced Christ crucified from their creed ? Apostates, who by their fall from grace had "crucified the Son of God afresh " ? No ! They were worldlings who had defiled the temple by their unseemly self-indulgences. And has the Lord no occasion to weep as he visits his church to-day ? And do his five bleeding wounds never plead in silent protest against what is done therein? I speak not of the one congregation into which he came in vision on that memorable Sabbath morning. The encroachments of secularism had advanced quite far enough therein to give occasion for sincere regret at their remembrance. But they were slight in comparison with what we have witnessed elsewhere.

"*Know ye not that ye are the temple of God, and that the Spirit of God dwelleth in you? If any man defile the temple of God, him shall God destroy; for the temple of God is holy, which temple ye are*" (1 Cor. 3 : 16, 17). We do not judge that the defilement here mentioned is that of personal impurity, in which one sins against his own body by the indulgence of fleshly lusts and passions. Though the words are often applied in this way there seems to be no good ground for so construing them. It is the corporate body which is spoken of, not the individual body; and to defile the temple of God is to profane that temple by bringing into its precincts idolatrous rights and ceremonies, secular and carnal indulgences, unsanctified amusements and frivolous entertainments to minister to "the lusts of the eyes, the lusts of the flesh, and the pride of life." Here we shall refer only to what we know as being carried on within the circle of Protestant and evangelical churches, confessing as we do so, that it is a shame even to speak of the things done by them in public. Nevertheless we must look at the unseemly catalogue : Performers brought from the opera or from the theatre on Sunday to regale the ears of the church with some flighty song of artistic musical display ; a star violinist dressed in the style of his profession, preparing the way for the sermon by a brilliant and fantastic solo ; a curtain drawn across the pulpit platform on a week-night, footlights and scenery brought from the play-house, and a drama enacted by the young people of the church, ending with a dance by the gayly dressed children ; a comic reader filling the pulpit on Monday evening, delivering a caricature sermon amid the convulsive laughter and hand-clapping of the Christians present. These are but a few acts in the comedy which the god of this world is performing weekly in church assemblies. Taken with the dramatic readings, literary entertainments, amateur theatricals, fairs, frolics, festivals, and lotteries, the story is enough to make the angels of the churches blush, and to give fresh occasion for an apostle's tears while he utters the solemn verdict : "For many walk of whom I have told you often and now tell you even weeping, that they are the enemies of the cross of Christ ; whose end is destruction, whose God is their belly, and whose glory is their shame, who mind earthly things."

It is well known that certain insects conceal

their presence by assuming the color of the tree or leaf on which they prey. Church amusements are simply parasites hiding under a religious exterior, while they eat out the life of Christianity. *Sacred* concerts, *church* fairs, *ecclesiastical* entertainments—how well the words sound in the ears of the unwary. But when the Lord appeared walking among the golden candlesticks with countenance like the sun shining in his strength, their real inwardness was instantly revealed. In the midst of the church entertainments, going on for the avowed purpose of winning the world into friendship with Christians; on the walls of the same church, inscribed in letters of gold, were texts of Scripture which the "dim religious light" had so obscured that few seem to have read them: "*If any man love the world, the love of the Father is not in him,*" and "*Know ye not that the friendship of the world is enmity to God?*" When the Lord came in, these inscriptions began to gleam out with such a dazzling brightness as the window panes sometimes exhibit under the rays of the setting sun. Then a great horror of being implicated in so-called sacred amusements seized upon one who read these burning texts, so that once on entering a church where such frivolities were going on, he hastened from the house as the aged Apostle John in Ephesus is said to have fled from the bath on discovering that the heretic Cerinthus was present.

If any shall name such scruples phariseeism or religious prudery, then come and let us reason together. Go into a Roman Catholic church and witness the services which are carried on there, and the question will at once arise, How is it possible that the simple spiritual worship of the primitive church could have degenerated into such a mass of grotesque ceremonials and idolatrous abominations as are here exhibited? The answer is easily found on looking into history. For a while the church was content to occupy the place of holy separation from the world appointed her by the Lord—witnessing for Christ, working for Christ, waiting for Christ. This austere attitude gave offense to the heathen who had often desired to be friendly with the Christians, and were ready to tolerate their religion if only they would accord some slight token of respect to their own deities—a gesture of reverence or a grain of incense. But all this was rigidly withheld by the disciples of Christ. Not the smallest concession would they make to pagan customs ; not a shred would they incorporate into their worship from the heathen ceremonials ; and so long as they maintained this spirit, they went forth conquering and to conquer.

Then, upon the enthronement of Constantine, the sentiment gradually changed, and the notion grew up that in order to convert the heathen it was necessary to conciliate them by conforming somewhat to their customs. The great Augustine also fell under this delusion, and gave his countenance to the engrafting into Christian worship of usages borrowed from the heathen. He said: "When peace was made (between the emperors of Rome and the church) the crowd of Gentiles who were anxious to embrace Christianity were deterred by this, that whereas they had been accustomed to pass the holidays in drunkenness and feasting before their idols, they could not easily consent to forego these most pernicious yet ancient pleasures. *It seemed good then to our leaders to favor this part of their weakness*, and for those festivals which they had relinquished, to substitute others in honor of the holy martyrs, which they might celebrate with similar luxury, though not with the same impiety.[1]" Here is the door opened through which the whole troop of abominations entered—saint worship, idol worship, virgin worship—till in an incredibly short time the church, which had gone forth to Christianize the heathen, was found to have become herself completely paganized.

The nineteenth century is presenting almost the exact facsimile of the fourth century in this particular. The notion having grown up that we must entertain men in order to win them to Christ, every invention for world-pleasing which human ingenuity can devise has been brought forward till the churches in multitudes of instances have been turned into play-houses, with theatre-

---

[1] Aug. "Epist.", p. 29.

boards announcing the courses for the gay season, boldly set up at the doors ; and there is hardly a carnal amusement that can be named, from billiards to dancing, which does not now find a nesting-place in Christian sanctuaries. Is it then phariseeism or pessimism to sound the note of alarm and to predict that at the present fearful rate of progress, the close of this decade may see the Protestant church as completely assimilated to nineteenth century secularism as the Roman Catholic church was assimilated to fourth century paganism?

And this is not all: the temple has been defiled. "For what agreement hath the temple of God with idols ; for ye are the temple of God : as God hath said, I will dwell in them and walk in them, and I will be their God and they shall be my people." Anything thrust into God's place is an idol. When, in 2 Thess. 2 : 3, 4, the culmination of the predicted apostasy is described, it is said of "the man of sin," that "He as God *sitteth in the temple of God*, showing himself that he is God." Here, I believe, we have a picture of the pope, thrusting himself into the seat of the Holy Spirit, assuming the title of "Vicar of Christ," which belongs only to that "other Paraclete" whom Jesus promised to send down to fill his place during his absence. This sin of unseating the Holy Ghost in his own temple is so blasphemous that its author has no forgiveness, but is doomed to be destroyed "by the brightness of Christ's coming." And is there no danger that Protestantism may fall under the same guilt? What if the Holy Spirit is ejected from the choir, and his office as inspirer of sacred song committed to a quartette of unconverted musical artists? What if he be unseated from the pulpit and the intellectual discourse substituted for that preaching of the gospel "*with the Holy Ghost sent down from heaven*" which God has appointed? What if he be set aside from the administration of the church, so that, for example, the settling of a pastor shall be made to turn on the votes of unconverted men called "the society," when the Lord has spoken about "the flock of God *over which the Holy Ghost hath made you overseers*"? Is there no peril that by this constant unseating of the Spirit he may be finally driven from his sanctuary, repeating as he retires the solemn lament of the Saviour: "Behold your house is left unto you desolate"? Wonderful indeed is the patience of the Comforter! As the Lord Christ, when "there was no room for him in the inn," condescended to lie in a manger, so the Lord, the Spirit, when crowded out of pulpit, and choir, and pew, and seat of authority, may retire into some obscure retreat of his church,—heart of humble saint or home of hidden disciple,—waiting patiently to be invited back to his rightful throne.

That he may, and sometimes does, finally withdraw from his temple, there can be no question. Do we not know of churches once fervently evangelical which are now lying under the doom of desertion by the Spirit? The writer thinks, with all charity, that he has seen such; churches upon which the Lord's sentence has gone forth, "Thou hast a name that thou livest and art dead." The body may still remain indeed, the creeds and Confessions may continue intact, and the forms of worship may even be multiplied and vastly "enriched" as the years go on, but these outward forms are only memorials of a departed glory, like the death-mask which preserves the mold of features which have long since crumbled into dust.

If any reader thinks that what we are saying is simply "exposition," we have to add that it is this and more; it is experience, and every word is confirmed in the mouth of heart-witnesses and conscience-witnesses and church-witnesses. When an evangelist goes to a congregation to hold special services, and finds after a day or two that the whole membership is in a state of suspended animation, let him take a candle, as the Hebrews did on the eve of Passover, and let him diligently search the house for leaven. Let him go into the choir gallery and learn whether a quartette of unsanctified musicians is seated there; let him then go into the vestry and inquire whether the winter's programme of church amusements is still proceeding. He may go farther, but the writer bears solemn witness that even these two obstructions have been found sufficient to bar the way to all success in revival effort. It is written and cannot, without infinite peril, be forgotten, that the church is "*an holy temple in the Lord*"; that it is "*builded together for an habitation of God in the Spirit*"; that "*the Lord is that Spirit*," governing and administering therein with sovereign authority, and that only "where the Spirit of the Lord is there is liberty." Except he has sanctified instruments in every part of the house, he cannot move through the assemblies in victorious freedom of service.

Yet, so inveterate is the tendency to turn away from the Spirit and to listen to other voices, that "He that hath the seven Spirits of God," warns his church from heaven in a seven-fold admonition repeated at the end of each succeeding chapter in her seven-fold apocalyptic history: "He that hath an ear let him hear what the Spirit saith unto the churches."

VII

CLEANSING THE TEMPLE

WHY not withdraw from the church which has become thus secularized and desecrated? To which we reply emphatically: Until the Holy Spirit withdraws we are not called upon to do so. And he is infinitely patient, abiding still in his house so long as there are two or three who gather in Christ's name to constitute a *templum in templo*, a sanctuary within a sanctuary, where he may find a home.

What the lungs are to the air the church is to the Holy Spirit; and each individual believer is like a cell in those lungs. If every cell is open and unobstructed the whole body is full of light; but if through a sudden cold, congestion sets in, so that the larger number of these cells are closed, then the entire burden of breathing is thrown upon the few which remain unobstructed. With redoubled activity these now inhale and exhale the air, till convalescence shall return. So we strongly believe that a few Spirit-filled disciples are sufficient to save a church; that the Holy Ghost, acting through these, can and does bring back recovery and health to the entire body.

I saw no whip of small cords in the hands of that pilgrim-Christ who turned aside for a moment to visit our sanctuary on that ever-remembered Lord's Day morning. The time has not yet come for judging and punishing those who defile the temple of God. On the contrary, it seems as though I heard that gracious stranger say: "Behold, I stand at the door, and knock: if any man hear my voice, and open the door, I will come in to him, and will sup with him, and he with me." The throne-room of the church where he has ordained to rule his flock; the choir-room where he would preside in the Holy Ghost as the inspirer of praise; the pew-rooms into which he would have freedom of entrance, even when coming in the lowliest garb; these he did not storm with violent anathemas, but gently solicited to open unto him. Woe to those who judge before the time! who depart from their brethren, and slam that door behind them before which Jesus is gently knocking; who spue the church out of their mouths while he, though rebuking it, still loves it and owns it and invites it to sup with him.

"For the law of the Spirit of life in Christ Jesus hath made me free from the law of sin and death," writes the apostle. This is the method of the Lord's present work—death overcome by life. "I cannot sweep the darkness out but I can shine it out," said John Newton. We cannot scourge dead works out of the church, but we can live them out. If we accuse the church with having the pneumonia let us who are individual air-cells in that church, breathe deeply and wait patiently and pray believingly, and one after another of the obstructed cells will open to the Spirit till convalescence is re-established in every part.

With the deepest humility the writer here sets his seal of verifying experience. When the truth of the in-residence of the Spirit and of his presiding in the church of God became a living conviction, then began a constant magnifying of him in his offices. Several sermons were preached yearly setting forth the privileges and duties of Christians under his administration ; special seasons of daily prayer were set apart, extending sometimes over several weeks, during which continual intercession was made for the power of the Holy Ghost. It was not so much prayer for particular blessings as an effort to get into fellowship with the Spirit and to be brought into unreserved surrender to his life and acting. The circle of those thus praying was thus constantly enlarged. Then gradually, the result appeared in the whole church ; the incoming tide began to fill the bays and inlets, and as it did so the driftwood was dislodged and floated away. Ecclesiastical amusements dropped off, not so much by the denunciation of the pulpit, as by the displacement of the deepening life. The service of song was quietly surrendered back to the congregation and, instead of the select choir, the church—who constitute the true Levites as well as the appointed priesthood of the New Dispensation—took up the sacrifice of praise anew and filled the house with their song. As noiselessly and irresistibly as the ascending sap displaces the dead leaves which have clung all winter long to the trees, so quietly did the incoming Spirit seem to crowd off the traditional usages which had hindered our liberty. Later came the abolition of pew-rentals and the disuse of church sales for raising money for missions and other charities. Meantime the pulpit acquired a liberty hitherto unknown; the outward hampering being removed, the inward help became more and more apparent, and the preacher felt himself constantly drawn out instead of being perpetually repressed as in the olden time. The prayer meeting soon passed beyond the necessity of being "sustained" and became the most helpful nourisher and sustainer of the church. The place is always filled, and instead of urging the people to come, or inviting them to participate, the attendance is joyfully voluntary, and the praying and testifying always so spontaneous and hearty that one can scarce rememember when it has been found needful to urge Christians to the exercise of these privileges.

It is by no means affirmed that the old leaven

has been completely purged out, so that nothing of the secular and unspiritual remains in the temple of the Spirit where we worship. No! If that Divine Visitant were to appear once more in yonder pew, and with those eyes which are like a flame of fire were to search our sanctuary, it pains me to think what he might discover, which has hitherto escaped our search. We are only speaking now of a comparative cleansing, deeply sensible of much, both known and unknown, which yet remains to be accomplished.

But of the result thus far may we speak without glorying. Most apt is Dr. Bonar's story of the auctioneer, who was commending in glowing words a picture by one of the old masters, himself meanwhile standing behind the painting which he was selling, and allowing it to hide him from view. All that we are trying to do in this chapter is to magnify the work of an "old master," the Galilean Carpenter, who only asked liberty to work among us that he might build "his own house; whose house are we, if we hold fast the confidence and the rejoicing of the hope firm unto the end" (Heb. 3 : 6). Let his work appear unto his servants, and let "the workers together with him" be hidden from view.

I observed neither saw, hammer, nor plane in his hand when he came into yonder pew on that morning; and though from that day he began to reconstruct the temple, "there was neither hammer, nor axe, nor any tool of iron, heard in the house while it was building." All went on noiselessly, so that now we wonder at the progress of the work.

One freshly anointed was moved to undertake a mission to the Jews, among whom up to this time no systematic effort had been made; the result—hundreds of Hebrews reached by the gospel, not a few converts won to Christ, and a Jewish missionary raised up for his people.

Another brother was drawn out on behalf of the Chinese; the result—a Chinese mission school of two hundred; twenty-five now members of the church, and one of their number, a veritable apostle, now returned to his native land, to make known the gospel to his countrymen.

A newly quickened disciple was drawn to the work of outdoor preaching; the result—a band of young men and women raised up who have gone to wharves, car-stables, and public squares, with increasing devotion to this service, which has now gone on weekly for more than five years.

Others were moved to enter into rescue work among ruined women; the result—a home opened and now a far-reaching effort extending out and bringing Christians of all names into co-operation.

An industrial home was instituted for intemperate and unemployed men; the result—a shelter in which thousands have found refuge, and converts have been won to Christ by hundreds.

A training school for evangelists was opened, designed to equip men and women of humble attainments for Christian work at home and abroad ; the result—a score of foreign missionaries sent out since the work began, four years ago ; and many more put forth into destitute fields at home, while a hundred and fifty are now under instruction.

Meantime evangelistic efforts have reached out on every side, some "tens" of our brethren being entirely occupied in this work and as many more working in the foreign field. By spontaneous free-will giving the offerings to foreign missions have steadily increased, rising to ten thousand, to twelve thousand, and one year to twenty thousand dollars, as the annual contribution to this work. And this increase in giving was not the result of begging or dunning. Much prayer was made and the strongest evangelical motive urged in behalf of it. Meantime there has been a freshness and heartiness in our worship hitherto unknown. The Spirit has had liberty to break forth in song in unexpected ways now and then, as when a joyous young disciple going down to be baptized sang the strains of "My Jesus, I love thee, I know thou art mine," as her feet touched the water, all the congregation uniting with overpowering effect. What could that little quartette box have done like this?

So, likewise, there has been an open window

into the sermon through which the Holy Ghost has come in with unexpected suggestions, fitted for the occasion. In a word, the law of liberty seems to have largely supplemented machinery and organization. And yet, be it noted, that even this record would not be committed to print save for one reason, viz., that it is recognized to be not a "work" but "his workmanship." Not one of these enterprises was planned beforehand, so that they could be credited to some superior organizer. They "grew up, he knoweth not how," who now tells the story. They are described after much hesitation, and with prolonged weighing of each statement, with the hope that they may bring home the suggestion to some who have not entertained it, *that the Holy Ghost, the present Christ, has been given to be the administrator of the church; and that in these days of endless organizations and multiplied secular machinery, he will surprise us by showing what he will do if we will give him unhindered liberty of action in his own house.*

PART III

THE DREAM AS INTERPRETING THE MAN

THE DREAM AS INTERPRETING THE MAN

THE preceding spiritual autobiography is based upon a dream. This is not the first time that a dream has proved a potent factor in a human life. Those who are familiar with the history of Catherine of Siena know how repeated and striking were her visions by day and by night; and readers of the life of Richard Baxter will recall his marked experience, and that vivid vision of lost opportunities which so quickened his after activity. Christmas Evans, also, that prince of Welsh preachers, while yet only a young convert and on the very night succeeding the loss of one eye from the assault of ruffianly violence, had a remarkable dream. He thought that the awful day of judgment had come, and seeing the world wrapped in its winding sheet of flame, he cried out, with mingled terror and confidence, "Lord Jesus, save me!" Then he beheld the Master turn toward him, and heard him say: "It was thy intention to preach the gospel; but it is now too late, for the day of judgment is already come." That vision of the darkness remained in the day so vivid a reality that the reflections which it awakened served to fan into a consuming flame of ardor and fervor his passion for souls. And he always believed that this and other dreams were God's messengers sent to communicate to him some of the mightiest impulses that swayed his life.

While, therefore, Dr. Gordon was not the first man, or preacher of the gospel, whose life, character, and conduct have been singularly molded by a dream, he was careful to claim even for this remarkable and unique experience, no supernatural origin.

"The prophet that hath a dream, let him tell a dream ;

"And he that hath my word, let him speak my word faithfully.

"What is the chaff to the wheat, saith the Lord."

In strict conformity to this divine injunction, this dream is told, as such, without affirming for it, or even implying in it, any authority. Nor is any philosophy here suggested as to those strange vagaries of the spirit in the semi-conscious state of sleep, which seem to belong to the borderland between insanity and inspiration, and which, after all these centuries, remain still an unsolved mystery. Yet, in this instance as in many others, the fact remains obvious that God has used a dream to put into life a new meaning, and impart to holy activity a new momentum.

There is one important law of dreams which should, however, be recognized : they do sustain an important relation to the habitual inner life. Whether by way of correspondence or of contrast, they serve as a sort of reflection of the mental moods and spiritual habits. Such a dream as is here recorded is therefore an index and interpreter of the man, and will bear careful study as a revelation of his inner self.

Dreams, moreover, have this unique peculiarity, that they translate the *historical* into the *poetical*, the *actual* into the *allegorical;* that is, they weave sensuous impressions or abstract ideas into concrete and often personal forms. The imagination, being no more restrained and corrected by the more practical senses, is left to itself to wander as it will and build fantastic forms unchecked by the sober realistic reason. Hence such a dream as is here crystalized into a narrative, when divested of its purely imaginative and allegorical dress, becomes a valuable exponent of the author's inmost habits of thought and feeling. As such we shall now consider it, believing these mental habits to supply the most helpful sort of practical and biographical commentary upon the striking narrative which was the last product of Dr. Gordon's gifted pen, and which forms the last legacy of this holy man and prince among preachers to the church of his generation.

The dream centers about the personal coming

of Christ to his own church, his reception there, the character of the worship he confronted, the fidelity of the gospel message he heard, the spiritual attitude of the hearers whom he met, and his general approval or disapproval of the whole atmosphere of the place of prayer ; and especially the measure of his recognition of the invisible presence and presidence of the Holy Spirit in the body of Christ. Who that knew Adoniram Judson Gordon needs to be told that such a dream is not a mere incoherent and senseless vagary of the mind, for it invests with poetic and allegorical form the ruling ideas and ideals of his whole later life, which may be classified somewhat as follows :

1. Loyalty to the person of Christ as Son of God and his own Saviour.

2. The blessed hope of his personal coming, as an imminent event.

3. The high vocation of the preacher as Christ's herald, witness, and ambassador.

4. The purity of worship as the exaltation of God alone in his sanctuary.

5. The supreme authority of the inspired and infallible word of God.

6. The conformity of entire church life to a biblical pattern.

7. The invisible presence and power of the Holy Spirit in the church as his temple and seat of administration.

To present these conceptions in their order, somewhat as they lay in Dr. Gordon's mind, and with impartial faithfulness, will be the simple purpose and purport of what follows ; and it is our hope that, in so doing, there may be presented a commentary on this dream ; and, what is even more valuable, an outline portrait, at least, of the man who is to be recognized as among the richest gifts bestowed by the Father of us all upon the church of this illustrious century ; and whose character and influence, all who best knew him desire to perpetuate and reproduce in the history now making for the august future.

I

LOYALTY TO THE PERSON OF CHRIST

"GO a little deeper and you'll find the emperor," said the wounded soldier of Napoleon's bodyguard, to the surgeon probing for the ball. And in the deepest soul of Dr. Gordon was the shrine of the personal Christ.

The genius of his whole godliness was found in this personal bond. He was jealous of truth of which all sound doctrine is the crystallization, and all true life the incarnation; but to him the living Christ was the Truth, and no mere creed could satisfy the soul that longed for a person to believe and love; and error was repugnant mainly because it meant a denial, or at least a dishonor, of Christ the divine Teacher.

This personal center of the gospel and of the new life explains all that is otherwise mysterious about this man of God. His conversion was his turning toward Christ as his Saviour and Lord. He believed the message that God gave of his Son, that in him is life everlasting, and that whosoever believeth in him shall not perish, nor come into judgment, but is passed from death unto life.

If he was not troubled with doubts about his own salvation, it was because he had learned, once for all, that the ground of hope is not internal, but external; not within us, but without us; not in any merit or works or feelings of our own, but in the perfect obedience and vicarious suffering of our great Substitute and Saviour. Instead of *trying*, he found peace in *trusting*, looking away to Jesus, as the Author and Perfecter of his faith.

It was said of Matthew Henry that, "when he lacked the faith of assurance, he lived by the faith of adherence." He, of whom we write, talked little of the assurance of faith, yet he never seemed to be darkened by doubt, because he walked in the light by the faith of adherence, which became to him the faith of assurance by unconscious transfer. When the hand has hold of another's hand, it is hard to doubt that other's presence; and if we thought less of our own assurance, and looked more to the maintenance of an assured and uninterrupted fellowship with a personal Saviour, we should know that we are in him and he in us by the Spirit which he hath given us, and by the constant and conscious touch of holy contact.

There is such a thing as Isaac Taylor, in one of his chapters on "Holy Living," calls the "Practice of the Presence of God." "Lo, I am with you always, even unto the end of the age," says the omnipresent Master; and there is no greater need than that this presence shall be recognized and felt. It cannot be detected by the physical senses, for it is not a sensible fact. But, to him who cultivates the sensibility to the unseen and exercises his inner senses to discern good and evil, the reality of the presence of Christ may become as indisputable as anything demonstrable by the bodily organs.

Such communion with a personal Christ assimilates character to his likeness. "Beholding as in a glass the glory of the Lord, we are changed into the same image from glory to glory."

The rapid transformation of Dr. Gordon into the resemblance of Christ was patent to all observers, most of all to those who most closely observed him and best knew him. In the home, where it is most difficult to show piety, his piety not only was shown but it *shone*. Nearness of approach often dissipates the charm that invests others; but no one felt such absolute confidence in his genuineness and godliness as those who had most chance to detect the faults and the blemishes in his character.

Our Brother Gordon combined the Pauline and the Johannean temperaments in one, the active and the reflective; the combination is rare, and implies an equally rare type of character. Again, he blended to an unusual degree the intellectual and the affectional. Most men whose minds are so intense as his, lack heart-qualities; they impress others as cold, giving out light but not heat, and so having little drawing power. This man beamed with the warmth of sunshine. You could bask in his rays. There was about him a benignity, a benevolence, that compelled recognition. Much as he was admired, he was most of all loved.

All this was a result of the intense love he bore to the person of Christ. Had he simply studied Christianity as a system of truth, he might have been a righteous man, exhibiting a cold conformity to righteousness, as a marble statue, rigidly symmetrical and frigidly exact, conforms to the standards of art. But it was only when, penetrating beyond all mere doctrine, he found the person of Christ and fixed on him his gaze of adoring love, that he became the good man, and, like his Master, went about doing good, attracting to himself such devotion that for him hundreds would even have dared to die.

This generation has furnished no other man, personally known to me, who in these respects so resembled Dr. Gordon, as did Theodor Christlieb, of Bonn. Born in 1833 and dying in 1889, in his fifty-seventh year, his life had run over almost the same length of time and cycle of history, and his views of truth were strikingly like those of his American contemporary, even to such minute matters as divine healing and the Lord's coming; and, like his American brother, he could say at the last, "I have not for an instant ever had the slightest doubt that I am an accepted sinner, and, if I have to take leave of all else, I shall never have to part from thee, my Saviour." Christlieb also sought to train students for the work of evangelism, and had the keenest interest in missions, as his well-known book on the subject attests. He was the opponent of rationalistic criticism, affirming that the one key to the word of God is not found in commentaries nor in the study of the original text, but can be given only by the Holy Spirit of God in answer to prayer. He, like Dr. Gordon, revered the pietists who had kept alive the slumbering embers of piety and missions amid the deadness of almost universal rationalism and skepticism. But most of all did these two men resemble each other in the blending of the active temperament of Paul with the reflective temperament of John, and in that intense loyalty to the person of Christ which made all other attractions fade and pale in his presence, as the stars retire at dawning of the day.

To a man, whose central passion was thus absorbed on the Christ of God, and who was accustomed to put Jesus before him in daily life, as the engrossing object of enamoring love, the standard of all excellence, the model for all imitation, the final Judge whose approval is the only verdict to be valued, it is not strange that a dream should crystallize about his divine Lord, and that the supreme question which that dream suggested was, "*What would Christ say if he came to church?*"

II

THE PERSONAL COMING OF CHRIST

THERE are three mountain peaks in the landscape of biblical history and prophecy, and each represents an *advent*. First, the advent of the first Adam, in the creation; secondly, the advent of the Second Adam, in his incarnation; and thirdly, the second advent of the Son of Man and Son of God, at his final revelation. Each of these peaks presents a double prominence; for the creation of man is associated with his fall, the incarnation of Christ with his death, and the second coming of Christ with his reign.

Between the first and second of these advents, stands one simple object, an altar of sacrifice fronting both ways and linking the two: for every victim that bled and burned on the altar pointed backward to the sin of Adam and forward to the coming Lamb of God. And between the second and third of these advents, the incarnation and the final revelation of Christ, stands likewise one simple object—the Table of the Lord, that likewise points both ways and links the two: for, "As often as ye eat this bread, and drink this cup, ye do shew *the Lord's death till he come.*"

There is something very beautiful about the simple faith that accepts the mystery of biblical teaching without hesitation, even where it defies penetration and explanation. Dr. Gordon was one of the giants of his day. Few men have minds more colossal in stature and more Titanic in grasp. Yet he bowed meekly to Scripture teaching, even where reason could not explore. The doctrine of the Lord's second coming, with the august events attendant upon it, such as the first resurrection of the sleeping saints and the rapture of living saints, the development and destruction of antichrist, the conversion of the Jews and the personal reign of the Son of God, the apostasy of the church, etc., presented to his mind difficulties and even discrepancies which his reason could neither unravel nor reconcile. But, having satisfied himself that the Bible is the word of God, he had no further question than this: What does the Bible teach? And as he found this truth lying on the very surface of the word of God, it would have been an irreverent rationalism either to refuse to receive it or to attempt by a tortuous exegesis to explain it away.

Inseparable from this biblical authority and prominence of this truth was its *naturalness*, as the completion and consummation of the divine plan. There is an unpublished and probably unwritten lecture of Dr. Gordon's, on the "Plan of the Ages," which those who heard it regard as one of the most masterly products of his study of the word, and in which he set forth the divine teaching as to the providential purpose exhibited in the course of history. In the Epistle to the Hebrews we find the grand conception that God made the "time worlds" ($αἰῶνα$) as he did the matter worlds, and framed them together like the joints of a body or the beams of a house; in this study of the ages Dr. Gordon carefully traced the teaching of the word of God as to these successive periods of history. He divided them into three: the Age of Preparation, the present Gospel Age of Ingathering, and the Age of Consummation; or the age before Christ, the age from his first to his second coming, and the millennial age. In a marvelous way he then proceeded to show how all prophecies, precepts, and other teachings of the word fall into their appropriate place when their relations to these three ages are understood; how countless difficulties are relieved and countless errors avoided, so soon as God's plans are rightly conceived. With the skill of a master, he then showed how, the moment that which is characteristic of the preparatory legal and Jewish age is imported into the gospel age, or what belongs in this present evil age is transferred over into the age to come, or reversely, we turn cosmos into chaos, and get everything out of order into confusion. A very intelligent hearer remarked, after a delivery of this grand address: "*Why you have just found a pigeon-hole for every text,*" and this well describes the practical effect of this study of the dispensational history of redemption. To Dr. Gordon the whole subject of the Lord's coming, however mysterious, seemed only the most natural event possible as the conclusion and consummation of the plan and history of redemption. The advent of man to this globe was also the signal for the disaster of sin and the ruin of the race. To repair this ruin the Redeemer came, but in disguise. It can now be seen that such disguise was essential to his mission, for had he come otherwise, he could not have accomplished his holy errand. Humiliation was necessary in order to vicarious atonement, for the Second Adam must be identified with the sin, sorrow, and misery of the race. He must be born of a woman, made under the law, "a man of sorrows and acquainted with grief." He must by his poverty and obscurity be identified with the lowest and the least, else how could he represent humanity as such ; he must be made sin for us, and suffer as a malefactor. All this implied an emptying of self—a making himself of no reputation, an obedience unto death. But surely this cannot be the *end*, the final manifestation of the Son of God. And so the word of God plainly reveals another advent, not in shame but in glory, not in disguise but in his essential investment, as the King of kings, with his proper royal retinue—the natural necessary consummation of the divine drama, the true revelation of the Son of God.

And the "blessed hope" has thus the highest prominence in the Scripture; it is revealed as the golden milestone toward which all events point and all roads tend. All good waits to find in his second appearing, his true epiphany, its completion and consummation. All that is best in human history is but the foretaste or first-fruits of which this is to be the harvest. The conquest of sin, now individual and occasional and exceptional, is then to be general, wide-spread, and final. Now, Satan, though resisted by saints, is yet at large working disaster to the race; then, he is to be bound and finally burned—consigned to the lake of fire. The Holy Spirit, now shed abundantly on believers, is to be poured out on all flesh. Evangelism, now like a river, with many little rills that reach far into the deserts and here and there turn wastes into gardens, shall then cover the earth with a flood as the sea does its bed. Now we see the outgathering of the elect from all nations: God visiting the Gentiles to take out of them a people for his name: then the very kingdoms of this world are to become the kingdom of the Lord Christ.

Christ's coming is to introduce events and developments of almost unprecedented character, such as the resurrection of sleeping saints, the restoration of Israel, the universal exaltation of God's anointed King, the final triumph of godliness, the judgment of God's enemies, and the reward of his servants.

Surely if the Bible did not reveal this as the ultimate outcome of the great historic ages, it would seem the most consistent and natural culmination and consummation of the redemptive scheme. This is the "blessed hope" toward which for many years our departed brother looked with unspeakable longing as the crown of all other hopes.

That which pre-eminently marks the Scripture teaching as to our Lord's second coming, is its *imminence*, or the combination of certainty at some time with uncertainty at what time. And our Lord himself made this imminence the main incentive to vigilance and diligence: "Watch, therefore, for ye know neither the day nor the hour wherein the Son of man cometh." To refer this to death is to violate the simplest laws of exegesis and upset the whole science of hermeneutics. Such, and similar expressions can refer to nothing less than the personal return of the Son of Man, to assume the sceptre and mount the throne toward which all prophecy and promise look. And as Dr. Gordon often said, there is not a virtue or grace in the whole circle or chorus of Christian attainments that is not in the Scripture connected expressly with this blessed hope.

This dream, therefore, not unnaturally pictures the Son of Man as coming suddenly to his temple—unexpectedly appearing in the midst of his people to test, as with refiner's fire, the service of his saints, as to whether or not it is an offering in righteousness.

III

THE SACREDNESS OF THE PREACHER'S VOCATION

THERE is one calling which especially deserves the name of the "High calling of God in Christ Jesus," namely, that of the preacher of the gospel. He who, from this divine vocation, goes into any other, though it be to occupy the throne of a world empire, steps down to a lower level. The piety and purity of a Christian community will therefore be found to be in exact proportion to the intelligent respect and reverence in which the office of the minister of Christ is held, and by which it is magnified.

Paul to the Ephesian elders,[1] gives the five-fold aspect of this office of the preacher and teacher: First, it is a *ministry of the Lord Jesus*, of whom he is a disciple and ambassador; secondly, it is a *ministry of the gospel of the grace of God*, of which he is a herald and witness; third, it is a *ministry of the kingdom of God*, in which he is a subject and representative; fourth, it is a *ministry of the church of God*, in which he is a servant and shep-

---
[1] Acts 20: 24-28.

herd; fifth, a *ministry of the Holy Ghost*, of whom he is an ensample, and overseer or bishop.

To Dr. Gordon the holy vocation was thus invested with this manifold opportunity and obligation, exalted privilege and commensurate responsibility. To fulfile these high functions, three things were pre-eminently needful: that the word of Christ should dwell in him richly, that Christ himself should abide in him, and that he should be filled with the Spirit. Hence he sought to know the word thoroughly as his text-book, to know Christ as his personal Saviour, and to know the Holy Spirit as his indwelling Guide.

He was, as became a preacher of the word, a man of clear and firm convictions. If physiognomy is any index of character, there was no mistaking the meaning of that large head, high, broad brow, firmly set lower jaw. It needed no exceptionally keen observer to detect and predict the intellectual capacity, intelligent habit, and courageous conviction, of which such signs were hung out by nature herself. And the signs were not misleading, for he lacked neither mental power, nor clear vision of truth, and tenacious hold upon it.

But this devout man of God had learned that it is not enough that one hold the truth, if the truth hold not him. " *Teneo et Teneor.*" How grand the significance of the metaphor in the Epistle to the Ephesians, which represents truth as the girdle of the warrior Christian—the very zone that, grasping the vital parts, holds all the other pieces of armor in place! But let us not lose sight of the fact that the minister of Christ must also know his Master, the living Word.

Thackeray sagaciously hints that there is a law of spiritual harvest; we sow a thought and reap an act; sow an act and reap a habit; sow a habit and reap a character; sow a character and reap a destiny. A character like that of Dr. Gordon is a whole history brought to light; it tells of habits of life, of thought as well as conduct, of a secret communion with God in the closet which shows its fruit and has its reward openly. Charles Lamb satirizes the man who vainly persuades himself that he can eat garlic in secret and not smell of it publicly. No man can walk with God in secret and cultivate the acquaintance of the unseen Christ, without character becoming radiant, until even his face will shine though he knows it not. Hence a minister is not only to be a herald but a witness. He is to tell what he knows, testify to that which he has tested and proved by testing, and, because experience limits his testimony, he must aim at a constantly richer and deeper experience in order to a witness correspondingly convincing and persuading.

How long will it take us to learn that power in service hangs on the height and breadth of attainment in divine things? A minister of Christ must be like a mountain, soaring high Godward into realms of unclouded faith and serene communion; for the higher his level, the surer and ampler the blessing he receives and conveys. The rains touch first the hilltops, and thence flow to the plains beneath, and the broader the hilltops the fuller and farther the flood. How can a congregation get a rich blessing from a pastor who does not live on a high level? The pastorates which have been most widely useful prove beyond doubt that he who, in the holy office, aspires to power, intense, extensive, pervasive, permanent, must first of all live close to God, and touch the very heart of Christ. He must hear by the ear in the closet what he is to proclaim with the tongue from the housetops. The higher the altitude, the richer the quality of the life and the life-imparting power. Fellowship with God is not to be sought only as a means to an end, for it is itself the end to which all means must contribute; but, when it is so sought and cultivated for its own sake and so found and felt as a fact of consciousness, he who enjoys such fellowship becomes the fountain of untold blessing to the church and the world.

Andrew Bonar, of Glasgow, shortly before his death, recorded this precious testimony: that from the time of his conversion, sixty years before, he had not passed a day when he lost access to the mercy-seat. Is it strange if he felt the power of Christ, as Paul said, canopying him, like the curtains of a tent?[1] The man who thus lives daily with God and in God, must live by faith. At such habitual heights, clouds and mists are left below, and the soul dwells in a clear atmosphere. How many soever the promises of God, they are all in Christ, yea, and through him, amen, subject to no discount, but like any sound financial paper, good for the full face value.

Our Brother Gordon likewise received, by a definite act of submission and appropriation, as he said to a few intimate friends, the *Holy Spirit as his guide*.

If any wondered at the simple trust which led him to attempt great things for God and expect great things from God, to undertake missions to Jews and Gentiles, drunkards and outcasts ; to build up a training school for evangelists and missionaries, and venture on God for the supply of every need, and, like Pastor Gossner at sixty years of age, stop ringing human door bells and knock only at heaven's gate—the solution is simple : all this mystery is unlocked by this one key—an elevated life of godliness, which can be understood by none who live on a low level, and a complete surrender to the Holy Spirit to be only a passive instrument in his hands. Dr. Gordon lived near enough to God to catch his own Spirit, which is love, unselfish, self-imparting love—that "royal law," or principle of life, nobler than any

---

[1] ἐπισκηνώσῃ

mere emotion or affection—which gives, gives all, and gives to all. Hence he not only preached the gospel to all he could reach, but he was essentially a missionary, for the Spirit of Christ is the spirit of missions. Foreign missions took passionate hold upon him because, like the love of God, they reach out toward those most distant and most destitute. His interest in the heathen, so far off, so needy, was largely involuntary. Because he was led of the Spirit and taught of the Spirit, he loved as God loves, and could no more limit his benevolent affection or beneficent activity to those near by him, than a full mountain stream could determine to flow only so far. If there is but little water that fact sets a bound beyond which the stream cannot pass; but the fuller and mightier the current, the broader the channel and the farther the onflow. Imagine the sun bidding his own beams bless only the nearest planets, and let Uranus and Neptune be bound in eternal night and ice! A Holy Ghost man never bounds his own effort by narrow limits, or by any limits. Rivers of living water flow from him and rays of divine light emanate from him, and to both there is no limit but the limits of human need.

The ambassador of Christ is so identified with his Sovereign that he may not only ask but claim his promised presence.

It is said by Williams of Wern, of Gryffyth, the Welsh preacher, that having to preach one night he asked to be allowed to withdraw for a time before the service began, and remained so long that the good man of the house felt constrained to send his servant to request him to come and meet the waiting congregation. As she came near the room she heard what seemed to be an indication of conversation between two parties, and, though in a subdued tone of voice, she caught the words: "*I* will not go unless *you* come with me." She returned and reported to her master: "I do not think Mr. Gryffyth will come to-night; some one is there with him, and I heard him say that he will not come unless the other will come also, but I did not hear the other reply, and so I think Mr. Gryffyth will not come either." The farmer, understanding the true case, replied: "Yes, *he* will come and I warrant the other will come too, if matters are as you say between them; but we would better begin singing and reading until the *two* do come." And sure enough when Gryffyth made his appearance there was another who came with him, came with him in power, and that proved a pentecostal meeting when many found newness of life.

The ambassador of Christ has a right to insist reverently on his sovereign Master's unseen presence and manifested power. How significant that prayer in the assembly of the early church, when, going out from the threatening council to their own company, the apostles with one accord besought God: "And now, Lord, behold their threatenings: and grant unto thy servants, that with all boldness they may speak thy word, by stretching forth thine hand to heal; and that signs and wonders may be done by the name of thy holy child Jesus"![1] Nothing takes away boldness in testimony to the Lord like the lack of his co-witness in his mighty works. He loves the reverent confidence that says, "I will not go unless thou go with me." If we are about our Father's business, we have a right to say: "And he that sent me is with me."

---
[1] Acts 4: 29, 30.

IV

JEALOUSY FOR DIVINE WORSHIP

AUL gives three marks of the true "circumcision"; and the first of all is this: the worship of God in the Spirit.[1]

These are days of especial peril from ritualism and formalism. This, which is the leaven of the Pharisees, is perhaps as dangerous as the leaven of the Sadducees, which is rationalism, or of the Herodians, which is secularism. Whenever, in the ages of church history, spiritual worship has declined, a formal devotion or at best a devout formalism has taken its place, and the forms of worship have multiplied in direct proportion to the lack of spirituality in worship. And so there are many who live close to God to whom the modern multiplication of ceremonies and rites is an utter absurdity.

An aged and venerable clergyman of the Anglican church, importuned by his son—who had run off into the extreme of a Romanizing ritualism—to preach in his "chapel of ease," at last reluctantly consented, but startled the congre-

---

[1] Phil. 3: 3.

gation by announcing as his text, "Lord, have mercy upon my son, for he is a lunatic," and then proceeded to show the utter lunacy of modern methods by which worship is robbed of all its primitive simplicity, of which an elaborate ceremonialism takes the place.

At an early period in Dr. Gordon's ministry, he began to turn his attention to the matter of public worship. The Saxon word itself gives us a most important hint, — *worth-ship*, — ascribing worth to God, describing his worth in terms most fitting and honoring to him, inscribing that worth on the door-posts and gates of his sanctuary not only, but on the gates and door-posts of our own dwellings, and the expanse of our brows, and the palms of our hands, as something to be constantly borne in mind.

The one supreme law of worship is this: "*The Lord alone shall be exalted.*" He is a divinely jealous God, in that he will have no superior or even *rival* in the affections of his people; he will not tolerate even as a medium of approach to him, anything whereby our thought and love are diverted from him. The ancient altar was to be of unhewn stone, lest the art expended in its adornment by the sculptor's chisel, might draw eyes from the vicarious victim that lay upon it. And so, in the house of worship, anything whatever which intrudes itself between the human soul and the object of worship is a fatal hindrance to the worshiper and a positive offense to God. Simplicity is of necessity the law of purity in worship, for it is the condition of singleness of mind. Elaboration, which is both the handmaid and offspring of art, may easily become idolatrous by introducing a type and style and standard of eloquence in oratory, of worldly excellence in music, of æsthetics in architecture, garniture, and furniture, which defeat the main purpose for which worship is instituted, namely, the exaltation of God alone before the fixed gaze of the soul.

This Boston pastor saw and felt what thousands seem unable to appreciate, or even apprehend, that it is not hostility to artistic perfection, but jealousy for spirituality, which inspires the purging of worship from secular attractions. No man who knew the pastor of Clarendon Street Church could accuse him of antagonism or indifference to the beautiful, whether in form or color or sound. He was no cast-iron utilitarian. But he felt the supreme need of a type of worship consistent with its divine conception and answering to its scriptural purpose. How could a choir of unconverted singers make melody in their hearts unto the Lord, or inspire holy harmony in worshipers? How could a musical performance on the part of mere artists, hired at costly prices, fulfill the high demands of public praise? He felt, and to this end he particularly wrought, that the hands which touch the organ keys, or the voices which sing psalms and hymns and spiritual songs, should be themselves at the disposal of the Holy Spirit, and usable as his instruments. Moreover, he felt that all worship must be marked by unity of impression. Hence a mere musical programme, arranged for artistic effect, without reference to harmony with the truth presented, and with other parts of worship, is an anomaly and absurdity.

This philosophy of worship he consistently carried out. It affected his preaching. He had early begun to study oratory as an art, and his aim and ambition were to excel in public address. The sermon was to be an ideal product, a finished work of brain and pen, delivered with grace and skill. But he found before long, that there is as much risk to the preacher in exalting preaching to a fine art, as there is to the singer in idolizing the æsthetic element in sacred song. To preach with wisdom of words has often made the Cross of none effect by hiding the crucified and glorified Christ behind the veil of human eloquence; and not until that elaborate and embroidered curtain is rent in twain from top to bottom, will the glory of God be revealed. It is possible to obscure the object of adoration by the very clouds of incense with which we surround him; to worship God with forms and methods which call so much attention to themselves as to forfeit all transparency and surround him with the opaque smoke from our own censers. The mere art of the apothecary has too much to do with compounding our incense, and in it are mingled too many earthly ingredients; there is too much smoke and too little fragrance.

Worship, in its wider scope, takes in all church conduct, even to the attitude of the worshiper, physical, mental, moral, spiritual. And the one law to keep before us, is this: "See that thou make all things according to the pattern shewed to thee in the mount (Heb. 8 : 5). Whatever is unscriptural is generally found to be unspiritual. The only way of avoiding a Romanizing ritual is to avert from our worship what is not enjoined or encouraged in the word of God. The spectacular involves risk, for it absorbs the attention through the eye; and the artistically musical, for it absorbs attention through the ear; whatever draws thought from God, hinders worship; whatever tends to lift him to sole prominence, by so much helps worship. And it is not too much to say that nothing which does not directly or indirectly contribute to such exaltation of God *has a proper place in sanctuary service.* Prayer and praise, the reading of the word and the preaching of the gospel, and even the offering of consecrated substance, are all, therefore, ways of exalting God, because they present man in the attitudes of suppliant and servant, student and steward, waiting at his Lord's feet.

How natural therefore, again, that our brother in his dream should searchingly inquire what would be the verdict of his sovereign Master were he to come to church, as to the reality or vanity of the worship he found there!

V

THE AUTHORITY OF THE WORD OF GOD

IF any two characteristics must always be inseparably associated with this devout disciple whose dream is here recorded, they must surely be his unshaken confidence in the *seven-sealed book of God* and his personal surrender to the *seven-fold power of the Spirit of God*. As to the book, that is a remarkable description or designation given us in the fifth chapter of the Apocalypse—the scroll, written within and on the back side, sealed with seven seals. What a striking metaphor to express the very handwriting of God in the inspired volume, attested with the seven-fold seal of complete authority and authenticity, and so bearing the unmistakable sanction of the divine Author!

The work will bear the marks of the workman—his knowledge and wisdom, skill and design. Moreover, the more perfect the workmanship the more complete the exhibition of the character of him who thought out and wrought out such perfection of product. Now it is very remarkable that just such seven-fold perfection is claimed for the word of God. We associate with him who is its author, seven attributes: such as omnipotence, omniscience, omnipresence—natural attributes; and providence, truth, righteousness, and love—moral attributes. All these his word displays in a remarkable manner and degree:

His Omnipotence, in the miracles of power which it records.

His Omniscience, in its predictive prophecies.

His Omnipresence, in its unity of plan and structure.

His Providence, in its history and biography.

His Truth, in its general accuracy.

His Righteousness, in its faultless morality.

His Love, in its transforming energy.

No survey of the inspired word is complete until it takes in all these forms of proof and methods of attestation and authentication. As it is of the utmost importance to us to know beyond doubt that the Bible is God's book, and to repose with absolute certainty upon its teachings, God has so fully set his seal and sanction upon it that no reasonable doubt remains. And it is significant that all these proofs of its divine origin lie *within itself*, so that we have only to search the Scriptures to find God's seven-fold seal impressed on them all the way through.

A. J. Gordon was the man of the book, and of the one book. No man, perhaps, of his generation, has done more in the line of Christian apologetics, but it was mostly by indirection. He defended the Bible by expounding it.

His attitude toward the Holy Scriptures was beautifully reverent. To him the Bible *was a living book*, not only containing a divine message, but divinely inbreathed, and therefore instinct with the divine life. As God first made man out of the dust of the ground, and then breathed into him the breath of life, so that man became a living soul, so, whatever was earthly and human in the book had taken form and fashion under the finger of God and had become living by the breath of his divine inspiration. This humble believer went to the Bible not as to a dead book, but as to a living being; he communed with the word as with a person, and expected to find in such converse the response to his advances and questionings, and he was not disappointed. He has often spoken of the word of God as giving answer, as one prayerfully searches it and seeks guidance in doubt, difficulty, and perplexity; and, in common with the most prayerful students of its mysteries, he found the heavenly Interpreter unfolding and applying its truths with the skill of a personal counsellor.

Dr. Gordon was not among those who doubt either the inspiration or infallibility of the divine word. He believed that it was essentially inerrant, and when he found difficulties or discrepancies, instead of distrusting the accuracy of the divine oracles, he rather suspected the accuracy of his own understanding. He traced the defects, not to the objects seen, but to the eye seeing ; and when contradiction was apparent, he waited, as when the twin pictures of the stereoscope fail to blend, one waits to get the common focal center of vision which resolves the discord into harmonious unity. In other departments of knowledge we understand in order to believe ; but in this divine science of spiritual mysteries we believe in order to understand. Faith is philosophy here, and obedience is the organ of spiritual vision : "If any man will do his will he shall know of the doctrine." "If ye will not believe, surely ye shall not be established."

To this constant and searching study of the word of God, our departed brother owed much of the energy and beauty of his writings.

In literary style he revealed remarkable power in analysis and antithesis, and these are perhaps the most conspicious features of his composition. He saw truth in itself and its relations. He had the homiletical faculty which detects the natural divisions of a text or theme as an astronomer sees orderly constellations where common eyes see only irregular and scattered stars. The facility and felicity with which he saw and expressed the elements of a complete truth, discriminated between things that differ, and arranged and adjusted related truths, were very remarkable.

He must have been a *clear* thinker to make such clear distinctions. There was no indefinite haze or indiscriminate muddle about his views or statements of truth ; and we cannot but think that he owed even these literary attainments largely to the daily study of His words who spake as never man spake.

A few examples may both prove and illustrate what we have said. In that remarkable book on "The Ministry of the Spirit," contrasting the work of Conscience and of the Holy Spirit, he thus represents the matter ; [1]

Conscience Convinces—	*The Comforter Convinces*—
Of sin committed ;	Of sin committed ;
Of righteousness impossible ;	Of righteousness imputed ;
Of judgment impending.	Of judgment accomplished.

He further says,[2] that "Conscience is the witness to the law ; the Spirit is the witness to grace. Conscience brings *legal* conviction ; the Spirit brings evangelical conviction ; the one begets a conviction unto despair, the other a conviction unto hope."

Who cannot see in such distinctions and discriminations as these the fruits of a microscopic study of the inspired word? The man who believed Scripture to be "literature indwelt by the Spirit of God" ;[3] that in the Scripture the Holy Ghost speaks, and "we can only understand his thoughts by listening to his words" ;[4] such a

---

[1] Page 202. [2] Page 191. [3] Page 173. [4] Page 176.

man would naturally examine into the exact terms used, and into the nicest shades of meaning which distinguish them from each other, and so learn for himself to use language with deep apprehension of its significance and critical accuracy in its application to the expression of ideas.

VI

THE SCRIPTURAL PATTERN OF CHURCH LIFE

"FOR see, saith he, that thou make all things according to the pattern shewed to thee in the mount." The church is a divine institution. It grew not, as many human institutions do, by a process of evolution out of man's conscious need. He who saw what man needed, fashioned this society of believers, and it was complete in all essentials from the first.

But, to tarry further on the thought of a scriptural pattern of church life, this dream reveals the whole secret of Dr. Gordon's purpose. He was not a dictator seeking to have his own way, and autocratically forcing on the church his own will; nor a half-crazy fanatic following some vagary or impracticable theory; but, like Moses, he had his eye on a scriptural and divine pattern, and he long and laboriously wrought to mold everything in church life according thereto. That a custom had grown up was no reason for its continuance; it might be, as Cyprian said, *vetustas erroris*. "Every plant which my Heavenly Father hath not planted shall be rooted up," said his Master before him, when his attention was called to the fact that his teaching had given the Pharisees offense. And the imperturbable spirit with which Pastor Gordon calmly went forward, without undue carefulness as to the opinions or opposition he encountered, in the pursuit of his object, must have been caught from his Master. He found some plants growing in the sanctuary courts which he knew his Heavenly Father had not planted, and he determined to root them up, though it might take twenty years to do it, as it did.

It may be well to ask, what are the *scriptural* marks of a church of Christ? They seem to be four: the apostolic church was an assembly for *worship;* an organized body for aggressive *work* for Christ; a *school* for training disciples; a *home* for the family of God. Doubtless all that vitally pertains to the original scriptural conception of a church of Christ can be included in this simple outline.

1. *Worship* was the leading idea, as we have seen, the exalting of God, and his dear son Jesus Christ, and the Holy Spirit, before the thought and adoring love of disciples. We find not a trace of sacred *places*, or sacred *persons*, and scarce a hint of sacred *times* or *seasons*. Wherever and whenever God and his worshiping people met, the ground was thereby hallowed and the time sanctified; and all believers seem to have been singularly on a level, preaching the word,

teaching the way of God more perfectly, and even administering sacramental rites.[1] Worship seems to have been perfectly simple, consisting of prayer, praise, reading and expounding the word, bearing witness to the resurrection of Christ, baptizing believers, and breaking bread in his name, with at least occasional offerings for poor saints. There are no clerical prerogatives, titled officials, choirs or hired singers, no secular trustees, no worldly entertainments, no consecrated buildings, and not a sign of a salaried service of any sort. God seems to be the center around which the early church crystallized, and the whole organization of believers was free from complicated methods and worldly maxims.

2. *Work* by all, in diverse spheres of activity, according to diversity of gifts, was the law of church life. The Spirit speaks expressly in the Epistle to the Ephesians,[2] that the very purpose of all offices and functions, apostles, prophets, evangelists, pastors, and teachers, was one sublime end: SERVICE. All the gifts and graces bestowed and distributed by the Spirit were for the perfecting of the saints unto the work of serving, unto the building up of the body of Christ, so that there might be the double growth of accession and expansion. The early church had no room for an idle and selfish soul. Every believer was a worker, warrior, witness. He came into the

---

[1] Compare Acts 8 : 4 ; 11 : 19-21 ; 18 : 26 ; 8 : 35-38.
[2] 4 : 11-16.

church as soon as he believed and was baptized, to be a member in the body where every member had an office, and must needs fulfill his function in order to the health and help of the whole body. The idea of simply coming into the church as a candidate for salvation has no place in apostolic ideas whatever. The church was composed of professedly regenerated people, giving themselves to the work of edifying saints and evangelizing sinners.

3. The *school* feature is prominent. The believer was a disciple, a learner, and he was to be docile and humble enough to be ready to be taught by any one competent to teach. In the majority of cases, converts needed instruction, and there is nothing more beautiful than where Apollos, the scholar and orator of Alexandria, puts himself under the tuition of two poor tent-makers of Corinth, one of them a woman, to be taught the way of God more perfectly. The first theological seminary was a humble lodging, with a single student and two professors, a man and his wife, and the wife the head of the faculty. Sublime simplicity indeed! where he that hears and believes enters a divine school, and takes his place as a pupil to be further taught whatsoever Christ has commanded, and trained to be a teacher and helper of others.

4. We must add to all these the conception of a *family home*. In order to become a radiating

point the church must be first a rallying point. There must be a bond of brotherhood and association in order to a mutual edification and an effective co-operation in service. And so we find love, the bond of perfectness and the impulse to all service, dominant in the early church. Love knows no distinctions, except it be in favor of the least and lowest, and love made everybody welcome and at home. Poverty and obscurity, ignorance and illiteracy, shut no convert out from sympathy and fellowship. Within the assembly of saints there were no caste lines or barriers. The idea of renting or selling pews or sittings at auction to the highest bidder—of setting up a property right and restriction in a place of worship, to make a poor man feel ill at ease or shut him out altogether—the very suggestion is utterly foreign to all New Testament notions.[1]

A preacher and pastor who thus magnifies his ministry in its five-fold relation to the person of Christ and the Holy Ghost, the gospel of grace, the church of God and the kingdom of God, as in every department simply a *service*, will communicate, consciously or unconsciously, the contagion of his holy enthusiasm to all receptive hearers. His preaching will be a university education in divine things. He will not think of his church as a *field* to work so much as a *force* to work with ; not as the parish which claims and

---

[1] Compare 1 Cor. 11 : 17-22 ; James 2 : 1-9.

bounds his love and labor so much as the garner containing the good seed of the kingdom, to be scattered for a harvest. He will try to train every believer into a herald and witness, so that from ear to heart and then from heart to lip and so from lip to ear again, the gospel message may run on its ceaseless round of salvation.

Because Dr. Gordon kept such a scriptural pattern before him and worked toward that, he gradually purged worship of all its meretricious secular arts, led his people into manifold forms of holy service, made the church literally a training school for disciples, and a home where poor and rich, high and low, met on terms of equal right and privilege. There was nothing for which he wrought which was not a part of the scriptural model, and he succeeded because he knew that God was with him and he could afford to wait God's time.

We can again understand the dream and its interpretation, for it is obvious that, in waking and sleeping hours alike, the question before him was, what would Christ himself say if he came to church? Would he find the assembly of saints exemplifying the scriptural and spiritual idea of the body of Christ?

VII

THE PRESIDENCY OF THE SPIRIT IN THE CHURCH

JOHN OWEN gave to the church a *Pneumatologia*—a discourse upon the Holy Spirit which, in his day, taught the church a much needed lesson. He maintained that each different age has its own test of orthodoxy. Before Christ came it was found in the attitude of God's people as to Messianic prophecy; in the day of Christ's personal incarnation, it was found in his reception or rejection by those to whom he presented his claims as Son of God; after the day of Pentecost the test was whether or not we have received the Holy Ghost, and how far he has freedom to work in and through us.

Adoniram J. Gordon, unconsciously perhaps, gave to the church another *pneumatologia*. He sought to realize for himself what it meant to be like Daniel, "greatly beloved of God"; and so he became in himself both an expression and exhibition of the fact of the Spirit's indwelling and inworking. From this personal experience he carried the doctrine and influence into the collective body of believers, and so sought to make the church of which he was pastor a living temple of the Holy Spirit.

This conception of the indwelling and presidency of the Holy Spirit affected two great spheres: first, his individual life; and secondly, his pastoral life. Personally he was so indwelt by the Spirit that he saw truth through illumined eyes. He was a seer, a modern prophet, in the sense of insight if not of foresight. In Samuel's days "there was no open vision," and the word of the Lord was correspondingly precious. Hannah's son was not only a Samuel, God-asked, but a Theodore, God-given—a special bestowment of the Lord to revive the spirit of prophecy and restore the open vision. A. J. Gordon was given of God to the modern church in the days of a waning spirituality, when the sense of the Holy Spirit's personality, deity, and even *reality* was dull and dim, and in some cases quite lost, to revive the impression and quicken the expression of the Spirit's actual and active indwelling. If he had any special office which was unique, it was to appreciate, and in his own person and life illustrate, the inworking and outworking of the Holy Ghost; and on a larger scale furnish both demonstration and illustration of the Spirit's administration of church life also under favorable conditions.

Upon this last and most important department of thought it is the less necessary to dilate, inasmuch as to it Dr. Gordon gives more than thirty pages in his work on "The Ministry of the Spirit."[1] But, for the sake of those who may not have read that masterly treatise, and to complete the interpretation of this dream, it may be well to sketch in outline the simple yet sublime conception presented in Scripture, and particularly in the Acts of the Apostles, of the Spirit's administration of church life.

Considered as a temple of which Christ is the corner-stone, and in which believers are living stones, he is the Divine Indweller, and holds there his throne and seat, as the Shekinah in the Holy of Holies of old. Considered as a body of which Christ is the head, and all regenerate souls members, he is the all-pervading and controlling Spirit that vitalizes and subsidizes the whole. The moment such a conception is formed in the mind, all the rest follows. He who is enthroned in a temple properly claims all homage and obedience; he who as the Spirit of Life fills and thrills the body, not only *may* but *must* rule in the whole organism, unless as in diseased members the conditions are so abnormal as to interrupt his proper activity. And again, as the spirit of life is the organizing power in the body, and distributes blood, nerve-force, nutritive energy in every part of the body, and, as the central will, wields for life's ends every member and organ—so the Spirit of God where he is permitted to control abso-

---

[1] Chapter vii.

lutely will make every part of the body of Christ both healthful and useful. If we *yield* he will *wield*.

Hence follow several vital conclusions:

1. As to the constitution and organization of the church, members should be added, and all officers should be appointed, by the Spirit. No ceremonies, ordinances, or sacraments can make a church-member any more than any human power can add a member to the body. We are to be jealous and zealous not to have multitudes added to church rolls, but "to the Lord." And, in electing officers, we are to look out those who have not only honest report and wisdom but are *full of the Holy Ghost;* otherwise how can he be unhindered in his administration? Every unregenerate or even unsanctified man or woman in a church office or even a church-membership, *obstructs* the *divine policy* of administration, so that we may virtually *unseat the Holy Spirit* from his rightful throne and "see," by putting into, or allowing to be put into, places of official trust, those who are not in sympathy with the Spirit's mind and methods. What then shall be said of the *invention* of a whole hierarchy, which borrows its entire framework from Constantine's imperial court, with a score of offices unknown to the apostolic church, with vestments and diadems, palaces and retinues, salaries and dignities; and what of the presumption of claiming to be the vicar of

Christ, when his ascension gift was his own Divine Vicar, the Paraclete! Is this not indirect blasphemy against the Holy Spirit?

We begin to understand now why this gifted pastor cared so little for ecclesiastical honors, dignities, and preferments. He yielded himself to the Holy Spirit, to be simply a servant—the servant of Christ and the servant of the church for Jesus' sake. All airs and assumptions of lordship were to him arrogant and offensive, and implied disloyalty to the Spirit. He was one of those of whom Hudson Taylor says that they are not so anxious to be successors of the apostles who went indeed to bring food but brought no inquiring soul back with them, as to be successors of the Samaritan woman who forgot her waterpot in her zeal to bear the living water to the thirsty souls at Sychar, and brought back a whole city to sit at Jesus' feet.

2. As to the distribution of spheres of service. Who is he that sets in the church, apostles, prophets, evangelists, pastors and teachers, elders and deacons and deaconesses; and appoints every servant for every service? Who knows the heart, and knows the work, and can fit each for the other, but the Lord, the Spirit? Of what transcendent importance to the church to have a divine wisdom select and a divine grace qualify every member for his own office; nay, to have the Spirit determine what work needs to be done, and what are the time, place, and way to begin it or

enlarge it ! What an awfully august privilege and responsibility combined, if it be possible and practicable for a church so to be surrendered to the Holy Ghost and dominated by him, as that in all deliberations and determinations, in all results reached through prayerful counsel and obedient self-surrender, it may be reverently true to say, "*It seemed good to the Holy Ghost and to us.*"

3. As to the practical purity and spirituality of church life. Temple of the Holy Ghost ! Body of Christ indwelt by the Spirit of God ! What a hallowing must there be to those who really believe this ! What a sad commentary on the church's attitude toward the Spirit, that it is possible without remonstrance for godless singers to be hired to conduct the service of song, which is a mockery without the grace in the heart that makes melody unto the Lord ! That it is possible in choosing a pastor, to consult only his intellectual standing and popular oratory, without ever asking whether he be a spirit-filled man ! That it is possible for such an unscriptural office to exist as that of secular trustees, and that men should be deliberately put into control without any regard often to the fact that they do not even profess to be regenerate !

There are some who cry down, by the obnoxious name of "pessimism," those who hint that the modern church is drifting toward apostasy. Yet what is apostasy but a *departure from the essential principles* of Christian life and church life! And Dr. Gordon, gentle as he was, and slow to accuse his brethren, felt in his soul that the church of Christ has largely lost sight of the very essentials of a Spirit-filled and Spirit-ruled body; and that Romanizing ritualism, rationalistic skepticism, and a world-assimilating secularism, are the trinity practically worshiped in the place of Father, Son, and Holy Ghost.

VIII

THE LAST MESSAGE TO THE CHURCH

DR. GORDON being dead yet speaketh. Perhaps some who would not hear while he lived will listen, now that he is no more among us, to the last message which he can ever deliver to his brethren.

What is the voice that breaks even the death silence?

1. He tells us that *preaching* is nothing if it be not the utterance of the mind of the Spirit, and that, therefore, we who speak must tarry long in the closet with the word, that he may unloose its seals and unveil our eyes to behold wondrous things out of his inspired book.

2. He tells us that *prayer* is the one vital element in all true worship, praying in the Holy Ghost, asking in Christ's name and by the power of the Spirit; the believer becoming the channel of a double intercession, the Holy Spirit interceding within by originating all true prayer, the ascended Christ interceding at God's own right hand, by receiving, perfecting, and transmitting all true prayer.

3. He tells us that *praise*, which is the element of worship apposite to *prayer*, needs a spiritual mind to appreciate and a spiritual frame to exercise it. Church music as a fine art simply, is an affront to God rather than an approach to him, for it assumes and presumes to set up an art standard in place of the beauty of holiness. There are two passages, respectively in the Epistles to the Ephesians[1] and the Colossians, which being combined, would read somewhat thus:

"Let the word of Christ dwell in you richly in all wisdom, and be filled with the Spirit; speaking among yourselves, teaching and admonishing one another in psalms and hymns and spiritual songs, singing with grace in your hearts and making melody in your hearts to the Lord." Thus combined, we get a little world of suggestive teaching in this narrow compass. We are taught that the *prerequisite* to all holy service in song is two-fold: rich indwelling of the word of God, and complete infilling of the Spirit; then our songs become a holy outpouring of a spiritual acquaintance with the word of God and the Spirit of God. Again, we are taught that the attraction of such song is found in the grace and melody of heart, which only God can detect or hear. But we are also taught a lesson, most unique and novel, that such song is a vehicle for mutual

---
[1] Eph. 5 : 19; Col. 3 : 16.

teaching, exhorting, admonishing. In other words, it is one way of preaching the gospel of salvation to sinners and of edification to saints.

How blind we have been that we have never understood the value of holy song as a means of teaching, reproof, correction, and instruction in righteousness, like the inspired Scripture, and of imparting wisdom, grace, strength, comfort, like the inspiring Spirit! Church music, purged of its secular corruptions and charged with the Spirit's life, might become spiritual food and drink, medicine and message, all at once; a feeder, healer, helper of souls. Is it that now?

The dream and the dreamer are left to us only in memory. But was not God speaking to the whole church when, in the visions of the night, he stamped on Pastor Gordon's mind and heart the image of *Christ coming to church?*

Let us judge ourselves, that we be not judged. Let us try our ways and turn again unto the Lord. Let us dare cease measuring ourselves by ourselves, and comparing ourselves among ourselves, and set up God's own standard of measurement and comparison.

"And the Lord said unto me, . . What seest thou?

And I said, A plumbline.

Then said the Lord,

Behold, I will set a plumbline in the midst of my people." [1]

---

[1] Amos 7: 8.

God is applying his standard to the work which men have builded, and its unhallowed and irregular construction is sadly evident. Who among us with the clearness of a divinely given vision, the courage of a divinely wrought conviction, will dare pull down what is not plumb and level by his standards, and rebuild according to the divine pattern?

Blessed temple of God, indeed, to which the Master can come and find no need of the scourge of small cords. Blessed church of which he can say:

"Thou hast kept my word,
And hast not denied my name.

. . .

I have loved thee.
Because thou hast kept the word of my patience,

. . .

I also will keep thee
From the hour of temptation." [1]

---
[1] Rev. 3: 8-10.

Phoenix Series

Something Wholly New and Wonderfully Good

Books by Authors of Proven Popularity

Books Excellently Printed and Durably Bound

Books at an Astonishingly Low Price

NOW READY

Beautiful Joe
That fine tale of an ugly dog

Dr. A. J. Gordon's
"Ministry of the Spirit"
and his
"How Christ Came to Church"

PRICE, 25 CENTS EACH
By mail, postage paid, 30 cents

Our Fall Publications

The Quiet King

By Mrs. Caroline Atwater Mason. Illuminated binding, fine illustrations.
A story of the Christ. Unique, eloquent, informing.

A History of Anti-Pedobaptism

By Professor A. H. Newman, of MacMaster University.
A book for all who want to be posted regarding an important movement in the Church.

The Hero of Start Point

and other stories   By J. MacDonald Oxley. Beautifully illustrated with illuminated chapter headings.
A book for boys. Splendidly suited for a gift book.

For the Other Boy's Sake

and other stories. By Marshal Saunders, author of "Beautiful Joe." About 250 pages, illustrated by 10 full-paged pictures.
These stories, with their strong human touch in them, will enhance this author's reputation.

Messages of To-day to the Men of To-Morrow

By Geo. C. Lorimer, D. D.   12mo. About 250 pages.
A series of papers by the eloquent pastor of Tremont Temple, especially adapted to young men.

Inspiration as a Trend

By D. W. Faunce, D. D.
A new view of an old topic. Timely and strong.

Thoughtful Books For the Thoughtful

* * *

Quotations of the New Testament from the Old
By Franklin Johnson, D. D. 12mo, 428 pages.
Price $2.00
One of the strongest and most scholarly books of the season.

The Argument for Christianity
By Geo. C. Lorimer, D. D. 12mo, 480 pages.
Price $1.50
One of the very best books on "Evidences" in existence.

Christian Teaching and Life
By Alvah Hovey, D. D. 12mo, 286 pages.
Price $1.25
Packed full with that which our people need to know.

Christ's Acted Parables
By N. S. Burton, D. D. 12mo, 256 pages.
Price $1.00
A new way of teaching an old subject.

The Ministry of the Spirit
By A. J. Gordon, D. D. 12mo, 233 pages.
Price $1.00
One of the richest books ever published.

The Spiritual Life
By Geo. C. Needham. 12mo, 262 pages.
Price $1.00
Inspiring and devotional.

Good Fiction for Reading People

Saxenhurst
A story of the Old World and the New
By D. C. Eddy, D. D.
12mo. 440 pages. $1.50
A most delightful story

The Temptation of Katharine Gray
12mo. 340 pages. $1.50
One of the powerful stories of the season

Judith's Journal
By Mrs. Janie P. Duggan
12mo. 364 pages. $1.00
Pleasant summer reading

Charlotte's Revenge
By Mrs. Caroline Starr Morgan
12mo. $1.25
A story of schoolgirl life

The Master of Deeplawn
By Hattie J. Colter
12mo. $1.25
A capital story of the evolution of a young man

Saved to Serve
By Harriet Cecil Magee
12mo. 378 pages. $1.25
Bright though not sensational, interesting and yet healthful

Fresh Things for Young People

The Mexican Ranch
By Mrs. J. P. Duggan.   12mo, 377 pages.

Price $1.25

A capital missionary story.

The Dawn of Christianity
By Professor H. C. Vedder.   16mo, 208 pages.

Price 90 Cents

Tells of the origin and growth of the Church.

The Parchments of the Faith
By Rev. Geo. E. Merrill.   12mo, 288 pages

Price $1.25

Shows how our Bible came together.

History of the English Bible
By Professor T. Harwood Pattison.   12mo, 281 pages.

Price $1.25

As fascinating in style as a romance; as full of information as a text-book.

Quick Truths in Quaint Texts
By R. S. MacArthur, D. D.   12mo, 336 pages.

Price $1.25

Full of suggestiveness and as breezy as a spring morning.

Booklets for the Time

Yachow and Burma
BY WM. M. UPCRAFT
12mo. 61 pages. Illuminated cover. Fully illustrated
A booklet full of interest and bristling with information

DIAZ—The Apostle of Cuba
BY KERR BOYCE TUPPER, D. D.
16mo. 32 pages. **10 cents**
A most interesting account of the great Christian worker

Divine Healing
BY F. D. PHINNEY
10 cents
An honest effort to test a doctrine by the Scriptures

Three Lectures on Missions
BY H. H. HARRIS, D. D.
20 cents
The Scriptural basis of Missions expounded

Talks to Baptist Young People
BY PROF. H. C. VEDDER
16mo. 59 pages. **15 cents**
A capital series of discussions on the Young People's Movement

The English Bible in American Eloquence
BY REV. THOMAS E. BARTLETT
16mo. 43 pages. **10 cents**
Very readable and helpful

Corner Stones of a Baptist Church
BY ALVAH S. HOBART, D. D.
16mo. 26 pages. **5 cents**
One cannot find anywhere a more compact exposition of the essential elements of a Baptist church

THE NEW YORK PUBLIC LIBRARY
REFERENCE DEPARTMENT

This book is under no circumstances to be taken from the Building

form 410